The New Era Lectureship, University of Southern California—Fifth Series

Some Exponents of Mystical Religion

By
RUFUS M. JONES
Professor of Philosophy in Haverford College

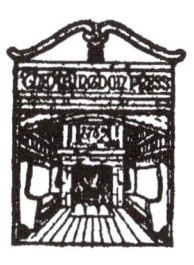

THE ABINGDON PRESS

NEW YORK   CINCINNATI   CHICAGO

Copyright, 1930, by
RUFUS M. JONES

All rights reserved, including that of translation into foreign languages, including the Scandinavian

Printed in the United States of America

CONTENTS

	PAGE
FOREWORD	5
INTRODUCTION	7
I. THE MYSTIC'S EXPERIENCE	13
II. PLOTINUS, THE FATHER OF WESTERN MYSTICISM	44
III. MEISTER ECKHART	80
IV. THE INFLUENCE OF THE MYSTICS ON MARTIN LUTHER	121
V. MYSTICISM IN ROBERT BROWNING	150
VI. THE MYSTICAL ELEMENT IN WALT WHITMAN	176
VII. MYSTICAL LIFE AND THOUGHT IN AMERICA	209

FOREWORD

NEW ERA LECTURESHIP FOUNDATION

THE Trustees of the University of Southern California established in 1919, in the School of Religion, a New Era Lectureship Foundation providing for a biennial course of lectures on subjects vitally related to present day development in religious life and thought, to be delivered by men of outstanding ability and reputation in the field of religion.

Previous lecture courses on this Foundation have been delivered by Bishops Adna W. Leonard, Richard J. Cooke, Francis J. McConnell, and Edwin H. Hughes. Dr. H. Wildon Carr, the widely known English philosopher, now of the faculty of the University of Southern California, followed Bishop Hughes.

The last course was delivered by Dr. Rufus M. Jones, the lectures comprising the content of this book. The conditions of delivering required a limitation in length of time and number of lectures, but the author has been free to make such changes and additions as he has thought advisable. The chapter on "The Mystical Element in Walt Whitman" was omitted for lack of time in the lecture course, but it is added in the publication.

JOHN F. FISHER, *Dean*,
    Schoool of Religion, University of Southern California.

INTRODUCTION

THE chapters of this book were given as a course of Lectures on The Modern Era Lectureship Foundation, at the University of Southern California in April, 1929. The opening chapter is a fresh attempt to reinterpret the nature and significance of mystical experience. It carries on and aims to clarify my position in this field of religion. The other chapters are in the main historical illustrations through great personalities of the meaning and value of the mystical approach to God. It is believed that each chapter adds something further to the interpretation of mystical experience given in the first chapter, so that the book is essentially one coherent whole.

I never find it profitable to enter into the confusions of religious controversy, and I never consciously do it. I feel a strong repulsion to the misunderstandings and recriminations that so often becloud the issues of the soul. But no one can stand for such claims of religious experience as I make here and elsewhere without laying himself open to a challenge from schools of thought that are fundamentally different either in basis or in emphasis. There are other ways of interpreting human experience besides the way which seems to me to be psychologically sound in principle and true to all the facts. I am simply concerned to strike this note of mine clearly and intelligently and then to let the "truth" of it be settled by the siftings and testings of time and thought. It is worse than useless to "press" in golf, and it is equally futile or defeative to try to establish "truth" by pressure or by intensity of emphasis.

I am especially concerned, in this period, when there is a keen and awakened interest in religion of the first-hand type, that the movement should develop along lines that are psychologically and philosophically true to our whole nature and at the same time in directions that give promise of enlarging scope and expansion of truth. There are interpretations of life which seem to fit the facts of experience, and in a superficial way do fit them, but which nevertheless are thin and lacking in prospective richness. There are other interpretations which reach down to the deeper levels of man's fundamental nature and take into account not only the surface currents but the ground-swell tides as well.

Much of our present-day philosophy of life ends in thinness and sterility because the creators and interpreters of it have been misled into the easy belief that all the issues of life can be handled by the same methods and the same categories that have worked with astonishing success in physical, chemical, and biological laboratories. Analysis, description, and demonstration are such potent and effective methods where they work that it is natural that scientific minded seekers should aspire to bring all the aspects of life under a single method and should feel little satisfaction in contemplating the looser and more inexact methods of valuation and interpretation. Why not be content to find God by the same route along which we find nebulæ and stars and atoms and molecules and germ-plasms? Why not climb continuously up the rounds of the ladder which science uses with such success and find the sphere of religion as an inherent part of that single unbroken system? Why make a jolt and a break and jeopardize religion by locating it in a special area of its own and by insisting on some peculiar inside route to it which is not on the scientific map?

The answer is that the scientific route invariably and necessarily leads only to objects that occupy space or that are capable of being mathematically determined. A universe reduced to a strictly scientific order is not our complete and infinitely rich universe. The scientific formulation squeezes it down to those dimensions and aspects that can be handled by exact methods of analysis and description and ignores all the aspects that do not fit those methods.

Those aspects of life and experience which we express in terms of personal intents and attitudes, of awe and wonder, of freedom and initiative, of joy and beauty, of love and grace, of inspiration and vision, of creative insight and flash of discovery, aspects by which we enlarge the entire range and scope of life, do not comfortably submit to the methods of science. We need poetry as well as fact. We need to achieve what has been called "imaginative dominion over experience," which produces greatness of life. None of us could *live* on the dry provender of analysis and description alone. A world that was only a "fact-world" with no visions of relief would drive us all into sheer insanity. If, as Shelley thought, we "stain the white radiance of eternity" by our many-colored dome of life, we just as certainly transform the many-colored concrete details of life by rising above the dull presented facts and by glorifying them with gleams of the eternal in the temporal. That "imaginative dominion over experience" not only makes poets and prophets, but it keeps the race sane and normal, and enables us common mortals to walk the earth with a serene joy in love and beauty. Until some one shows how the scientific ladder, that is nothing but a scientific ladder, climbs up into the regions of unselfish love and beauty, we may well continue to insist that there are values of life which must be approached and appreciated by other ways of apprehension than those which are appropriate for discovering atoms and nebulæ.

Religious experience is as unique in quality, and it rises as certainly above the mere fact-level as does love or beauty, but it calls for other methods of interpretation and valuation than those which are adequate for space-time objects. I am not defending a two-world theory nor am I urging that there is a break or chasm between facts of science and values of life. I am only contending that our world, and especially certain aspects of it, overbrims the methods and categories of exact mathematical description, and leaves a precious overplus by which we live and move and have our being as men. It is not two worlds we are talking about, but, rather, two ways of apprehending our one world. What peculiarly comes to light in these value experiences is the depth and range of the mind—the inner self—of the beholder or the interpreter who has the experience. He reveals himself to himself in all these matters as not just one object among other objects, but as a creative spirit able to rise above the level of facts and the array of things, and to partake of a realm of life which is of a higher spiritual order than that of atoms and molecules.

I am endeavoring to show that human experience at its richest and best reveals this overbrimming life and guarantees to us a world of being which is kindred to our spirits.

I

THE MYSTIC'S EXPERIENCE

I suppose there is no question that we should all lose our faith in the reality of the external world if we entirely lost our contact with it through sense. If eyes and ears, touch-sense and "muscle-sense" all went dead and made no reports, the world would fade away like a dream. We accept much about the world, no doubt, on the testimony of others, but we could hardly stand the mental strain of losing all our own first-hand experience of real things. The mystic feels that same way about the reality of God. He welcomes the testimony of others about God and the revelations of former times, but he wants the *conviction* that can come to him alone from his own experience of God. He wants to be able to say with the aged Saint John, "I have seen with my eyes, and my hands have handled."

"Experience" is a very loose word and may mean almost anything or nothing in particular, and the word "mystic" too has a strangely varying gamut, ranging all the way from highest reality to lowest rubbish. I shall use "experience" to mean the firsthand, direct-contact approach to reality as distinguished from the later, more matured processes of the mind in thought, dialectic, logic, and reasoning. It is a distinction between what William James called "knowledge of acquaintance" and "knowledge about," and what Hegel called "implicit" knowledge and "explicit" knowledge.

The distinction is, I admit, somewhat artificial, since we can hardly talk intelligently of "knowing," or of having "knowledge," until we have taken some mental steps to mediate, think through, relate, and comprehend what was "given" to us in our experience of so-called first-hand acquaintance. If we stopped absolutely with the flash of pure sense-experience and refused to go on and interpret it in terms of our wider, larger consciousness, through memory, association, imagination, and thinking, we could *say* nothing about it. We could give it no meaning. It would be like "a grin without a face." And yet everybody recognizes the fact that all our knowledge of the external world is embedded in and, in the last analysis, rests back upon these multitudinous intuitions of sense-experience of ours. It is through them that we get our stock of knowledge of acquaintance. And it is also through them that we acquire our data for interpretation.

The word "mystic," as I shall use it, stands for a person who insists on a somewhat wider range of first-hand acquaintance with reality or of direct experience than that which is confined to the operation of the five or more special senses. The special senses have become organized, through slow evolutionary processes, for dealing practically with concrete objects in space. They enable us to get adjusted to what we call the external world, and they make it possible for us to feel at home in it. There is an immense area of mystery still attaching to sense-experience. The mystery is often "hushed up," or glibly passed over with words and phrases that are supposed to explain it. But, as a matter of fact, nobody knows how we make our contacts with the world outside our minds. There is no satisfactory theory that explains how we pass over from molecular vibrations outside the mind to consciousness of color and form and objective reality grasped and possessed inside the mind. The mind somehow on the occasion of a signal makes a flash, or a leap, of interpretation of the signal. And, behold! "we know an object."

The "mystic," as I was saying, carries his range of acquaintance a little further than the common sense-experiencer does, though his increase of range does not make the situation any more mysterious than it already was in the field of sense. The mystic believes, in fact, feels himself forced to believe by direct evidence, that the mind has other ways of first-hand acquaintance than through these special senses. It seems to him that the mind by its own inherent power can make a flash or leap from within and feel itself in contact with spiritual reality of the sort that does not occupy space as the objects of sense do. The mind is, quite certainly, always self-transcendent even in the field of sense experience; that is to say, every time it apprehends an object of sense it leaps beyond itself and lays hold of what it did not possess before and could not have conjured up out of its own "substance"—out of its own empty hat! It goes beyond itself.

The claim of the mystic would be, then, that in mystical experience the mind comes into immediate contact with environing spiritual reality, somewhat as in sense-experience it comes into relation with objects in space. There is quite obviously nothing inherently impossible or improbable about this claim of the mystic. Experience of spiritual reality which is kindred to the nature of the mind itself would seem *a priori* to be more natural, more to be expected, than the other type of experience would be which has given us our familiarity with what we call "the material world," that in many ways seems alien to the mind.

The process of arriving at this latter world is, as we have seen, no less mysterious than the process of leaping to a world of spiritual reality. It comes back in the final resort to a question of actual *evidence*. If we all experienced the world of inner reality in the same conviction-compelling way by which we are forced to admit noises and colors and weights and resistance through the "bombardment" of our senses, and if, furthermore, we could interpret this inner spiritual world in universal terms so that we could transmit our experience to other people and have it mean to them precisely what it means to us, there would be no more skepticism about spiritual reality than there now is about the world that we learn of through molecular vibrations.

It must be admitted at once that the "evidence" which mystical experience supplies of contact with an inner realm of spiritual reality is not of a sort that can be interpreted in universal terms to the same degree as the objects of sense can be interpreted, and, consequently, the testimony of the mystic does not convince others in the same way that, for instance, the scientist's testimony to the existence of atoms does. For the mystic himself, however, the experience of God does often possess that *conviction-compelling power* which attaches to sense experience of external objects. It is more like the quiet joy one feels in the presence of exalted beauty, or when listening to music that fits the inner mood of the hour, or in the moment of the discovery of the meaning of love. These are all incommunicable experiences.

They cannot be universalized as information about the stars can be. And yet the conviction-compelling aspect of these experiences is often greater than anything we ever get from the external world of atoms and molecules. There is a crude but expressive phrase which puts this conviction-aspect very well. We say, "I feel it in my bones," when we are as certain of something as we are of life itself and yet we cannot prove it by an appeal to facts that stand forth for universal inspection. It is what my late friend A. Clutton-Brock used to call "the soul's scent for truth." It is a "homing-sense" like that of the migrating bird. The mystic by a flash of inner insight feels an infinite depth of more Life than his own lying under the surface currents of his finite self. We can truthfully say of any person who takes his soul seriously what Wordsworth said of "the six-years' darling of a pigmy size":

"Thou whose exterior semblance doth belie
Thy soul's immensity."

Without more debate or discussion, at this stage, about the objective evidence of the mystic's experience, let us turn to see what this knowledge of acquaintance has meant to some of those who have had it. There is no complete Baedeker for the wayfarer to use; no maps or charts or ladders of ascent that are effective for everybody. But those who have "been there" flash considerable light back on the trail, and they tell us "how their bones felt" as they went up the steep ascent of the soul or down into that bottomless depth which lies under our thin surface life.

The great "prophets" of the race, that is, the creative spiritual leaders and builders, have usually been rich in the quality of their knowledge of first-hand acquaintance. The "scribe" is satisfied to reinterpret what some one in an earlier time discovered. He is essentially a backward-looker. He prizes authority, tradition, the august prestige of antiquity. He has slender faith in the fundamentally divine capacity of the soul. The oracles of the present time are for him dumb. The revelations of truth are all hoary with age. The mystic, on the other hand, speaks what his own soul *sees*. He is a present revealer. He has the assurance of a mighty first-hand conviction. Amos, one of the most rugged and downright of the world's prophets, came to the people of his time with the words, "The Lord God hath spoken, who can help prophesying?" He says again and again, "Listen, for I saw." Isaiah leaves no doubt in any reader's mind that his message to the nation has come up out of a great living experience that seemed to him a theophany. "I saw God" is his awe-inspiring announcement. "I had my lips touched with a burning coal of fire that cleansed my being," is the substance of his claim to speak with authority. Jeremiah, one of the greatest figures in the entire history of the religion of Israel, stood the pathos and tragedy of his nation's downfall, and the agony of persistent misunderstanding, because he was throughout the hard period of crisis upheld by the certainty that his mouth was touched by the hand of God and that he was the human voice uttering a message that came from beyond himself.

It is not too much to claim, I think, that wherever in the course of history religious life and thought have had a fresh new birth, have surged up with a new intensity to a higher level and have brought release of new power to live by, there has always been at the heart of the movement a leader of the creative type, whose insight came from knowledge of acquaintance. Mystical experience is more or less transmissive and contagious, as all experiences of intensity are likely to be. There are *birth-times* in the progress of all religions. After periods of dullness and apparent exhaustion there come mysterious periods of gestation and rebirth, and the onward moving wave rises to a new crest. Sometimes there is more than one creative leader who shapes the line of direction. But whether it be through one or many that the release of energy comes, it will generally be found that the reality of God has freshly and powerfully broken in on the consciousness of the dominant personality or personalities.

All that we know of Gotama Buddha gives the same impression of his life and mission that we get of the greatest prophets. There is a quality of depth to his life and to his words that carries a weight of reality beyond what we attach to one who merely learns wisdom from everyday experiences of the world. He had lived his way down below the surface-life and seems to speak out of eternity, as all supreme prophets and spiritual creators do. I feel the same way toward Confucius. He was for the most part of his life certainly not a mystic. His way of life as it developed in Chinese history would appear to be strikingly non-mystical. And yet there are passages in the writings of Confucius, as they have come down to us, that indicate an inrush and uplift of life that carry him far beyond his cautious, practical moralizing. His remarkable countryman Moh-ti, who came perhaps a generation later, was distinctly of the mystic-prophet type. Moh-ti threw away caution and utilitarian schemes and proposed to his people to *live dangerously*. He was one of the first persons in any country to rise to the full insight that God is love, and that life can never be rightly lived until men learn to love as God loves. There has, too, always been a very live strain of mystical faith running through the history of Mohammedanism, and it has been conclusively shown by recent scholars that Mohammed himself belongs distinctly in the order of the mystics. He was on many occasions exalted with the consciousness of the Divine Life invading him. There was a mystic quality in all these leaders of the faith of great racial groups, and they were all conscious, in their sublimest moments of vision and insight, that they were drawing their truth from eternal springs.

This first-hand experience of God marked the entire life of Christ. The book of Acts calls him "the pioneer of life," and the Epistle to the Hebrews says that he was "the pioneer of faith." His leadership in both these aspects was beyond doubt due to the fact that he was in his own experience the *pioneer in the discovery of God as Father and in the insight that grace or self-giving is the divine way of life.*

Our generation with its fresh historical insight has been coming to see that Saint Paul, the second founder of Christianity, the man who carried the gospel of Christ to the western world, was primarily a mystic rather than a theologian. His interpretation of Christianity was plainly enough based in the first instance on his own experience rather than on the historical tradition which he received from others. "Paul an apostle (not from men, neither through man, but through

Jesus Christ, and God the Father, who raised him from the dead)" (Gal. 1.1), is his fiery challenge to those who were insisting that the sacred system of the past was to be an essential feature of the Christian way of life and salvation. It would be difficult to find a more positive assertion of firsthand experience than this: He who said, "Let there be light," hath shined into my heart to give the light of the knowledge of the glory of God in the face of Jesus Christ (2 Cor. 4. 6).

The Ægean cities and the district of south Galatia, where a large part of Saint Paul's life-work lay, as a missionary of the new faith, were at this period areas of a certain type of mystical thought. A slow invasion of Oriental faiths had been creeping into these regions for at least a hundred years. It was mysticism of a somewhat primitive form, such as became familiar under the names of mystery religions and Gnostic faiths, but they were all characterized by this peculiar mark that they believed the soul of man to be of divine and heavenly origin, and that salvation would be granted only to those who were initiated into a secret, unutterable experience through which the soul could recover anew the original divine powers that had been smothered out by being immersed in the flesh and in the material world.

There is not much evidence to show that Saint Paul borrowed anything of real importance from this seething, semimystical environment in which he lived during the most constructive years of his missionary labors. But there is no doubt that his hearers were quick to respond to the mystical note in his message and were in a state of mind that made them ready to travel in the direction in which the great apostle was himself predisposed to move. The interesting result was that Christianity began its career in Europe profoundly charged with a mystical element.

Saint Paul's own new life felt to him like *a new creation*. Something more than "energy" or "power"—which were his favorite words—had come into play within him. There seemed to him to be a creative, transforming spiritual presence operating in him. Sometimes he calls this creative presence within him "God," sometimes "the Spirit," and sometimes it is given the designation of "Christ" or the "Spirit of Christ." The word varies; the fact remains. He used the phrase "in Christ," or "Christ in us," a hundred times.

No quotation of scattered passages can convey in any adequate way the remarkable interior depth of this spiritual conqueror of the Græco-Roman world. The historical setting of the battles is often alien to our age and the modern reader who has not taken pains to become familiar with the issues of the first-century struggles often feels somewhat confused as he reads, but there are an extraordinary freshness, a virility and a rugged reality to the central figure in these spiritual battles. But beyond all other traits and qualities of his complex character stands out the unplumbed depth of this man's soul. "It pleased God through his grace to reveal his Son in me," is his astonishing claim. It is his continual aspiration to "know the *power of the resurrection,*" to attain to the "measure of the stature of the fullness of Christ," "to know the breadth and length and depth and height," and "to be filled unto all the fullness of God." A few of his sayings will indicate how far he is removed from the rabbi or the forensic theologian and how completely he is allied with the mystical type of person who *knows* by *acquaintance*. "It is no longer I that live, but Christ lives in me" (Gal. 2. 20). "Beholding as in a mirror the glory of the Lord, we are transformed into the same image from glory to glory even as from the Lord, the Spirit" (2 Cor. 3. 18). "I can do all things through Christ which strengtheneth me" (Phil. 4. 13). "We are more than conquerors through him that loved us" (Rom. 8. 37). "The riches of the glory of this mystery . . . which is Christ in you" (Col. 1. 27). "Ye also are builded together for a habitation of God in the Spirit" (Eph. 2. 22).

One does not need to turn to Greek sources of influence to explain the mystical strain in Saint Paul. It is fundamental to his nature and not derived from outside sources. Western Christianity was essentially mystical at its birth. This mystical element is no less striking in the Christianity of Saint John. Next to Saint Paul he was the greatest first-century interpreter of Christ—greatest, we may as well add, in any century. The influence of Saint Paul is clearly in evidence in his thought. Christ has become for him the Spirit of truth, leading and guiding men from within into all truth. He is the Bread of Life. He is the eternal Fountain of living water springing forth in the soul. He is the living Vine, pouring his vitalizing sap through all the human branches that are organic with his life. He is the Way, the Truth, the Life. Saint John puts a strong emphasis on the deeper, eternal world that everywhere lies behind the visible one and that breaks through and reveals itself in the midst of time in responsive souls. We usually associate this point of view with Plato, and it may well be that there is a Platonic tinge in the heart of Saint John; but, if so, it was so inherently a part of his being that he was unconscious that he had drawn water from Greek wells. Saint Paul before him had learned to "look not at the things which are seen, but at the things which are not seen; for the things which are seen are temporal; but the things which are not seen are eternal." If that is Platonic, it is almost certainly unconscious Platonism, and was a part of the vital air that great souls breathed in the first century.

In any case the idea of an eternal, invisible world within the world we see was woven into the original web of Christian thought in the apostolic age. Christianity started on its course of spiritual conquest not merely as a religion built around a great historical Figure. It was from the first profoundly mystical, insisting that the Divine Life, revealed in the Christ of history, is constantly being born anew in the hearts of believers.

Historical mysticism has had many stages and many varieties through the centuries, and many writers on the subject have been so much under the spell of a type of mysticism which centers on ecstasy as the goal of mystical experience that they admit no other type to be worthy of the name. Ecstasy is a rare and unusual experience. It comes only to persons who possess a peculiar psychic constitution, and when it comes it is ineffable, unutterable. So far as words are concerned, or thoughts or ideas, it is a blank —a time-gap. The soul is "caught up" into a state that transcends all known human experience. It is called the *via negativa* be-

MYSTICAL RELIGION

cause only by negations can the recipient of this experience say anything about it—"it is *not* this;" "it is *not* that."

The mysticism of Saint Paul and of Saint John is very different from this negative, abstract type, so different that many interpreters of the New Testament have not suspected that the original stream of Christian life and thought was saturated with mystical experience. It seems to me that we are thoroughly justified in giving the word "mysticism" a wider meaning than that of the ecstatic and ineffable type. It is a form of religion that builds primarily on consciousness of acquaintance with God through direct and immediate experience of him, instead of on logical and forensic arguments about him, or on a scribal interpretation of ancient records that tell of him. Religion of this deeper and more intimate type has through all the centuries, however "dark," or "medieval," or "scholastic," flowed on beneath dogmatic system and ecclesiastical structures and sacerdotal forms, like the rivers Abana and Pharpar deep down under the city of Damascus.

The volume of the stream of mystical life

has always been much larger than the books about it would indicate. Where there has been one mystic who has put his experiences into literary form there doubtless were a thousand who had the vision but who did not write. Elijah the prophet assumed that he was left alone as the only true worshiper in Israel and the only one who could hear the still, small voice of God in the inner deeps. But he was told that God's account of the faithful is different from man's account and that there were seven thousand devoted souls in a land where Elijah was confident that he was the only representative of spiritual religion. So it often is. We count the short roll of famous mystics, and we conclude that they are peculiar, rare, and more or less solitary individuals, and we forget that the records of the inner life of man are very incomplete.

> "Hearts that are fainting
> Grow full to o'erflowing,
> And they that behold it
> Marvel and know not
> That God at their fountains
> Far off hath been raining."

The whole spiritual level of life in unheralded communities has again and again been raised by some mystic who wrote no autobiography.

At periods of awakening or rebirth in the life of the church the submerged stream has broken through and become more evident. Sometimes the "inspiration," the kindling spark, has come from Saint Paul or Saint John in the New Testament, sometimes it has come from Plato or Plotinus, sometimes it has been Saint Augustine of Hippo, or that mysterious Eastern mystic who made the world believe in earlier ages that he was Saint Paul's convert in Athens, "Dionysius the Areopagite." But in actual fact, if we obliterated the mystical strand from the story of Christian life and thought, we should alter that story beyond all recognition. The heart has had its romance as well as the head its logic, and the worshiper, burning with love and fervor in the consciousness of the real Presence, has certainly been as much a part of Christian history as that great intellectual feat of constructing the creeds of Christendom or the building of the imperial church has been.

We come here to a vital question which

has often been asked and which calls for a fresh answer. Is this so-called mystical experience something which is granted to a few favored souls by a special act of the grace of God, or does it spring from a fundamental capacity of the human spirit? The former alternative would make it a supernatural gift. It would be an *addendum* gratuitously made to man's natural capacities. Those who have the gift would be the chosen few, "whom God whispers in the ear." With the Augustinian conception of man as lost, fallen, ruined, depraved and utterly devoid of spiritual quality, that supernatural view is the only one that could be legitimately held. Not only must the mystical gift be conceived as supernatural by the Augustinian, but "saving faith," as well, had to be thought of as a divine favor conferred upon "the elect." We should remember that Saint Augustine's theory of man's nature is no more "sacred," and no more proved to be a true theory by his saintliness, than was his theory of the heavens circling about the earth as a center. Canonizing him a "saint," as he deserved to be canonized, does not confer upon him infallibility in the sphere of truth.

The truth will be in the end as it really *is* and not as some good man *thought it was.*

Meister Eckhart, in the fourteenth century, took the position, as we shall see more fully in a later chapter, that the soul of man has an unlost and inalienable *Apex,* or *Ground,* as he sometimes called it. It is a Spark of God, a point in the soul that never has been and never can be sundered from God, for it partakes of his nature. It is something in us that is a common meeting place between the soul and God. It is a little Shekinah which we all carry about here in our wilderness wanderings, and those who learn how to recollect and withdraw from the turmoil and din of the world and come back into the stillness of this Shekinah are instantly with God, and his Son comes to birth in them. As soon as a person "comes to himself"—comes all the way back to the ground of his being—"God must of his own nature," Eckhart says, "give himself to that person and flow into him." But that noble view of Eckhart did not square with the orthodox Augustinian conception of man, and the official church did not consider Eckhart "sound." He was undoubtedly following a trail which he got from the Aristotelians—that the higher active reason in man is a divine endowment.

A modern thinker who accepts evolution as the method of creation finds the Augustinian account of man no longer tenable. He does not approach any of the deeper problems of life or the world with a conception of man as a "ruined" or "depraved" being. On the contrary, for me at least as a modern thinker, the "emergence" of man in the order of life has introduced a being who is essentially spiritual, and not a mere collocation of atoms or an aggregation of protoplasm. Something actually real in us is always missed when anyone attempts to reduce us to "naturalistic creatures," that is, to beings who are to be explained by physical forces alone and solely in terms of cause and effect. There is something in us that transcends space and time and matter and mechanism. They are *for us* and not we *for them*. The organizing, interpreting principle is in us. The center of mind from which we look out and read the story of the world is forever something unique and original. One does not arrive at it by raising matter and plant or animal to their highest potency. We create as well as receive. We see beyond what is given. We live all the time in reference to a world that is not yet. We see a row of facts and under our creative workmanship, presto! there suddenly appear *values* where before there were only facts. Beauty and truth and goodness and love have broken into the world we inhabit, and *they are here because we have come.* We are ever not quite "ruined." We are ever not quite "naturalistic." When *we* came something that belongs in the order of spirit arrived and set to work. We are, in the words of Saint Paul, "a colony of heaven"—poor, weak "colonists" perhaps, half starved, badly clothed and poorly housed and fed, but we partake of the future more than of the past, and we reveal dimly what man is to be and ought to be.

My main point is that reason, or spirit, is the central feature of our being. We can be "silly" and we can go "crazy," but when we are normal we rise above the "naturalistic order." We face life with visions of what ought to be. We fling a halo of values around our facts. We organize all our sense experiences with unifying, more or less permanent, mind-forms. We enlarge the whole range of life in ideal directions. Only rational spirit can do that. Matter is what it is. Spirit is what it proposes to be! What it expects to be!

That kind of a creative center man is, or at least some of us believe that we are. That kind of a spirit already belongs in a sphere that is supertemporal and superspatial. We belong to the spiritual order. We are *here,* but at the same time we are *beyond here.* We possess the capacities of spirit. That means that with all our feebleness we are in God's world and are, in absolute truth, "made in his image," partakers of his spiritual order of being; and if that is so then, "Spirit with Spirit may meet." Eckhart would seem to be right when he said: "God is as near to us as we are to ourselves." It does not seem to me in any way improbable that the deeper Life of God lies underneath our human spirits. It may be that we are more like Damascus, with its underground rivers, than we suspected. It is not at all unlikely that the eternal is the real, that the infinite is the ground of the finite, that the "seen" has come out of the invisible, and that our truest environment, after all, is spirit. Mystical experience, therefore, would seem to be something which the universe in its wholeness and entirety, has produced as much as it has produced goldenrod or columbine, for we have not dealt with the universe in its completeness until we have included in it the spiritual ground, the noumenal reality, that has made the universe a *universe,* and man in the full sense *man.* As Wordsworth put it, we

"must sink
Deep—and, aloft ascending, breathe in worlds
To which the heaven of heavens is but a veil."

I would hold, no less emphatically than the Augustinian believer would, to the gift of the grace of God in all high experiences of the soul. Only I cannot admit limits and bounds to that grace. The fact of free grace is written all over the face of the universe. Grace is a cosmic affair, not a penurious thing. Atoms and molecules and germplasms preach it no less loudly than evangelical ministers do. There is a wideness to it more expansive than the wideness of the sea. It would be strange indeed if at last at the pinnacle of creation it should turn out that only a small group of *élite* and elect souls were within the area of God's love, or could become the recipients of his grace! The failure in our communion and correspondence with God is due, I am sure, not to a limitation of love at the point of transmission, but, rather, to a dullness of heart at the receiving station. The universe is a vast broadcasting system and has always been vibrating with radio-waves; we have been very slow in learning how to "listen-in" and read their meaning.

Still slower are we in our response to "the deeper world" within the world we see. We are supplied with powerful instinctive driving-forces which have to do with here and now. We are swept with great emotions which bear upon the things we see and touch and hear. The vociferous noises of the outer world din our ears. The very drive of the urgency of survival has compelled us to bend our energies to learn how to get well adjusted to the world of space. We have, consequently, been slow and late in learning how to correspond with the other environment which is always fringing the margins of this "bank and shoal of time." "That is not first which is spiritual, but that which is natural; and then afterward that which is spiritual." (1 Cor. 15. 46.) Some day in the unfolding processes of life we shall learn to live inwardly as well as outwardly, and we shall breathe and grow in both worlds, as "higher amphibious" beings should do.

But it is an eternal law of life that there can be no *compulsion* in the realm of the spirit. It is essentially a world of free creative choices. The principle of freedom is as august as the voice of duty is. Emerson said once in a memorable passage: "Into every intelligence there is a door which is never closed, through which the Creator passes." I think it would be truer to say that there is a door there which we at any time *may open,* like those

> "Magic casements opening on the foam
> Of perilous seas."

It is possible, however, to be too absorbed in other things to hear the gentle knockings; it is possible to have too "static" conditions at our receiving end to hear the currents of the Spirit, though they are as close to us as breathing. *Expectancy* is an essential attitude for such correspondence, as it is for everything that concerns the deeper life of the soul.

> "Hope that can never die,
> Effort, and *expectation*, and desire,
> And something evermore about to be."

The Spirit comes not in the din of thunder, the roar of the storm, or the crash of the earthquake, but in a voice of stillness which must be listened for and which calls for an alert and cultivated hearer.

The word which I wish to say at the end is, that the experience of God which surges into the mystic's consciousness seems to him its own evidence of God. It carries with it the same *sense of reality* that attends the perception of mountains or the sound of oncoming trains of cars. The psychologist may analyze the experience and reduce it to a state of subjectivity. The mystic will quietly answer: "It was not my real experience that you analyzed. You were dealing only with an abstract mental state of a general class and not with my concrete experience with its inward depth and its transforming power." The physicist may say, "We know of nothing that can be called real in the universe that is not made up of masses of matter in motion. Your 'experience' is nothing but an effect of molecular currents that streamed through a given area of your brain cortex. It is no more an evidence of God than the burning of a lump of coal is." The mystic answers that, though "the words are strong," they amount only to a sheer dogmatic statement. There is no evidence for the assertion. There is not a scrap of proof that thought is an effect of matter. All we know about matter is known through thought and until the end of time—and afterward!—thought will be the *prius*, the presupposition, of everything else.

The mystic will not be scared by the proclamations of materialism. Until some one comes who can "rail" consciousness of acquaintance "off the bond," and make experience nonexistent, the mystic will go on enjoying his glimpses of the Life that is and he will continue firm in his faith that his soul and God stand sure.

II

PLOTINUS, THE FATHER OF WESTERN MYSTICISM

Emerson boldly declared in his poem, "The Problem":

> "One accent of the Holy Ghost
> The heedless world has never lost."

"One accent" means, of course, "not one accent." It looks at first sight like an Emersonian exaggeration of optimism, but more things are conserved in this universe than we might have guessed from the testimony of our crude senses. Along with the law of the conservatism of matter and of energy there may possibly run also a law of the conservatism of spiritual values.

Plotinus is rather a fine illustration of the fact that the seemingly heedless world will not let a great spiritual interpretation die. There have been long periods of history when his name was known to only a few experts, when most of his teaching was attributed by name to Plato or to Aristotle or to some one of his disciples, but during the last hundred years he has been slowly emerging from the semidarkness which enveloped him and he is now taking his place with the five or six greatest thinkers of all the ages. It can be shown, I believe, that very few men have ever lived who to the same extent have shaped the thought and colored the spiritual experience of the Western world.

It seems pretty clear that no other single person outside the New Testament group and outside the group of early Christian Fathers contributed so much to the stream of Christian thought as Plotinus did. Indeed, many of the "Fathers" were debtors to Plotinus. If the church had consciously known how much it owed to this "outsider," it could very properly have conferred upon him the title of "saint," but it was a case, as so often happens, where the "borrowing" is not recognized, and where consequently no obligation is felt to "pay back" in the form of honorary degrees.

Plotinus not only produced the type and brand of "Platonism" which became current in Christian circles in western Europe, but he also became one of the major intellectual influences in Asia, and his thought colored both Christian and Mohammedan philosophy in the Near East. When Arabic mysticism came up from Spain into Christian circles, in the early thirteenth century, in the Mohammedan commentaries on Aristotle, it was found to be Aristotelianism fused with the teachings of Plotinus in just about the same proportion as Christian mysticism in orthodox circles was fused with his ideas. Men in both these world religions who never heard the name of Plotinus were living on spiritual bee-bread that came from his hive. In some strange way the task was conferred upon this man from Alexandria to gather up the precious spiritual legacy of Greece, to remold and adapt it into the proper form for absorption into the life and thought of Christianity and to pass it on as nourishing milk and honey for ages yet unborn.

Plotinus was one of those Janus-faced persons who, on their narrow isthmus of time, looked both toward the past and the future, and formed out of their virile thought a living bridge between the great dead and the great unborn. He understood Plato far better than Aristotle did, though Aristotle had the advantage of having almost twenty years of intimate fellowship with Plato in the Academy, while Plotinus knew him only through his books. It is one more shining instance of the law that like knows like. What is more remarkable than the correspondence with the past is the way Plotinus anticipated the unknown future and worked out a system of life and thought which was to feed the souls of the greatest builders of the Christian Church. Cromwell used to say that a man never goes so far as when he does not know where he is going! Plotinus, like Abraham, went out not knowing whither he went, and he too became the father of a great spiritual family—like the sand of the sea for multitude, a family that is still expanding.

Plotinus, whose name is Roman, was born in Egypt, not far from Alexandria, about the year 205 A. D. Porphyry, his enthusiastic disciple, wrote his biography, but there are many details missing, since Plotinus was very reticent about divulging facts which concerned his mortal life, and Porphyry was at best a poor biographer. Plotinus would not have his portrait painted nor would he allow his birthday to be celebrated with festivities. He was not proud of the fact that he had a body. He shared in a mild degree the ascetic drift of the time which was everywhere in evidence, peculiarly so in North Africa. He was, from his early youth, a passionate seeker for truth, but he failed for the first twenty-nine years of his life to find any satisfactory guide. Some one by a happy chance suggested Ammonius Saccas to him, and he found in this new teacher the long sought guide. Ammonius, whose second name, "Saccas," means "porter," was a self-taught workingman. He must have been a unique genius, for he left a profound stamp not only on Plotinus, but on Longinus and on that great Christian scholar Origen as well. After ten years of discipleship under this inspiring master of wisdom, Plotinus seized the opportunity of gaining contact with the far East by joining the military expedition of the Emperor Gordian. The expedition came to naught and Plotinus had a narrow escape for his life, but he may quite well have enlarged his horizon by the journey, and he may possibly have felt some streams of Oriental influence which he would not have found so readily in Alexandria. His philosophy is essentially, however, the logical development of the highest level of Greek thought as found in Plato and Aristotle, but there is apparent in him an extraordinary religious intensity, a passion for the experience of the divine and a flight from the temporal to the eternal which are more truly characteristic of the East than of the West. At the same time there is little more evidence of an Oriental strand of influence in Plotinus than there is in Plato, in spite of the cosmopolitan character of third-century Alexandria as compared with the Athens of the fourth century B. C. It is not difficult to believe that the entire Platonic movement carries a strand of Oriental thought hidden at its heart.

Plotinus settled in Rome in 244, where he spent the remainder of his life as a successful and beloved teacher. Amelius, who had previously been a follower of Numenius, and Porphyry, his biographer and editor, were his two most famous disciples. He was a friend of the Emperor Gallienus and he gathered around himself a devoted fellowship of men and women. In spirit and character, Plotinus presents many of the finest traits of a saint. He remained, however, definitely outside the Christian fold. He must have had some contacts with Christians both in Alexandria and in Rome, but he never once mentions Christians nor reveals any consciousness of their views of life, though his silence is an active rather than a passive one. He spent much time refuting the contemporary Gnostics and setting forth their errors, but he allows the main stream of Christian thought to flow by without a single positive reference. He was fifty years old before he began to put his profound thought into writing, but he left behind at his death, in 270, a large body of literary remains which Porphyry sorted out, organized with some systematic care and arranged in six sections, consisting of nine "books" in each section, for which reason they were called "Enneads," or "Nines." The thought is compact, the style is difficult, and the student of Plotinus needs, as Socrates would say, to be a "Delian diver" in order to bring up the truth which the master buried below the surface in his tough Greek sentences. But there the treasure is, in very certainty, for the bold and patient seeker who is not afraid of hard labor. There are occasional passages of great beauty in the Enneads, though on the whole it can truthfully be said that Plotinus is one of the most difficult persons to grasp and understand of all the major thinkers that have ever lived, and at the same time he is the most worth knowing of the entire list of thinkers between Aristotle and Kant.

There are many ways of testing greatness. One sure way to discover the measure of a man's greatness is to find that the world will not let him die. If his thoughts become the necessary air men breathe, we may take it for granted that he has come upon something that is essential to human nature. If his ideas recur age after age in the fundamental strands of human thought, it may be assumed that he plumbed in an unusual way the deeps of man's mind. And if his highest experiences become pattern experiences for successive generations, that indicates a unique range of life in him.

I have emphasized, and shall continue to emphasize, the philosophical system of Plotinus—his way of interpreting the essential realities of the universe—but his immense influence upon the western world was due even more to the mystical element in his life and thought than to his intellectual system. He was, like Socrates and Plato, a person who belonged in the order of the prophets. He *saw* as well as thought. He *felt* the significance and value of truths that baffled and eluded his intellect. He had overbrimming experiences of realities that transcended his dialectic and his categories. Flashes and glimpses of truth that "broke through language and escaped" counted heavily for him. He had moments of experience of the type which J. A. Stewart has called "transcendental consciousness," and which Doctor Bucke named "cosmic consciousness." However we name them, they were moments when the below and the Above, the here and the Yonder, the finite and the Beyond, seemed suddenly to meet and fuse into a living One, an indivisible Whole, as a sensitive magnetic needle might lose itself and find itself in the enveloping current of magnetic energy surging out from the central sun and coursing through it. Plotinus was in any case a sensitive spiritual organ. The margins of his personal self were more pervious than they are in most men. Something came in, or something went out, that linked him inwardly with the reality that his thinking could not reach. Without actually traveling anywhere with his feet or by ships he felt that he had arrived at the Goal of his journey, "the haven where the pangs of homesickness are no more."

Four times, Porphyry says, Plotinus attained this Goal of life during the period that Porphyry was living with the master. "He kept his own divine spirit unceasingly intent," his disciple says, "upon the inner Presence." "He was pure of soul," the same biographer says, "ever striving toward the divine, which he loved with all his being." He showed, we are told, the most remarkable power of "going to the heart of a subject," and when he spoke "his face became radiant and illuminated." On one occasion he was seen to be enveloped in light. One of his fine phrases was, "strike and become a light to men." This he certainly did himself. He showed powers of contemplation that seemed to Porphyry "more than human"—in fact, contemplation was the secret of his life. It is not easy to tell why some persons are so much better organs of the life of God than others are. Perhaps, however, it is no more mysterious than is the fact that some substances are vastly better conductors of electricity than others are. In any case, Plotinus has raised in the minds of men through the centuries a greater faith in the inner pathway to God than did any other person who lived in the period between Saint Paul and Saint Augustine. Dean Inge says very truly that "the temper of this Neoplatonic saint was serene and cheerful, confident that the ultimate truth of the world was on his side," and he finished his earthly life saying, "I am striving to give back the Divine in me to the Divine in the All."

We have in Plotinus a mystic of the intellectual type rather than of the emotional type. His mysticism is not due to some accidental psychic trait of his nature. It is as far removed as can be from emotionalism or sentimentalism. It springs out of and completes his intellectual quest. It forms the apex of his dialectical movement. He goes up the ladder of his intellect to the last round of it, and then he finds that there are wings at hand for the rest of the journey. No one else to the same extent has made the mystical way an inherent feature of his entire philosophical system. The soul natively seeks to return home to God because in its origin it has come from him and it is always "bound by gold chains" to him. Everything that constitutes the spiritual universe belongs together in one undivided unity. The soul never *goes out* from God to the extent of leaving him behind. Nothing that is real can be sundered from God nor can anything real ever perish.

For Plotinus the universe consists of three grades of reality. It is a three-story universe. We can begin our account of it either from above or from below. There are a way up and a way down. There are a centripetal and a centrifugal movement. The universe has emerged, flowed out, or "emanated" from its Center, and the true way of life is to return again to the Origin. But we need to be very careful not to confuse and spoil the deeper meaning of Plotinus' interpretation by carrying over into it our persistent way of seeing everything in an external framework of space and time. "Out" and "back," "up" and "down," "before" and "after" are only figures of speech, only human symbols, which our "clay-shuttered" minds employ when we are describing another kind of world than the one of ultimate reality—the one Plotinus is talking about.

The three levels of reality are (1) the Source, which is the Alpha and Omega of the universe; (2) the Realm of Mind, in which are the forms and patterns of all that is; and (3) the Over-Soul, in which are all the vital creative energies of the world. The two lower orders overflow or overbrim, from the superfullness of the Source or Ground of all reality. This Source Plotinus calls the One, or the Godhead. He means by the One not a number in a number-system—not a mathematical figure. It is, rather, the absolute Unity of all reality, the apex of the pyramid of Truth and Goodness and Beauty. Back of all manifestations there must be a *Source* or *Ground* of the manifestations. This Ground out of which everything emerges cannot itself reveal itself, come forth and be expressed any more than the hidden self in us, behind or beneath our thoughts and our thinking, can by any possibility become an object of experience for us or for anyone else. It eludes us and escapes all our mental processes, though it is presupposed as the *prius* of them all.

All our human thinking and all our striving after goals of life spring out of a stratum in us deeper than our thought, a stratum which is the subsoil of our ideas and purposes. How they flow out we do not know. Even in finite beings like us the principle of the ground-source of mind and soul is taken for granted, without which nobody could be an intelligent person. There is a *one* in man as surely as for Plotinus there is a One in the universe—a spire-top junction which holds subject and object together in a higher unity, and which binds our many objects of experience together into an integral whole, without which we could neither think nor act rationally. So too, in the universe there must be some Unity more complete than that of subject and object as they are related in the knowing mind; there must be a One beyond the divisions of the many; there must be a Root from which everything has sprung; there must be a Godhead out of which all that is true and beautiful and good—that is, all that is divine—has emerged into being and into manifestation. "Everything that comes to be must of necessity derive," Plotinus says (*Enneads* III, 8. 9.), "from One that does not emanate, but is the *Principle of Emanation, of Life, of Intellect and of the Universe.*" "This," he adds, "can be no 'thing' among things, but must be prior to all things."

Religion, if it is to be more than a form or convention, demands something in God which rises majestically above our finite powers of comprehension. The moment God is leveled down to the plane of our understanding, and is thought of as a greater Object among other objects, religion ceases to have any unique scope or function. We are always in danger, in our emphasis on divine immanence, of merging God into the vague blur which we call the whole of things. We incline to bring him so "near" and "familiar" that all our reverence, awe, and wonder dissipate and fade into the light of common day. The soul needs in God not only something near, something warm and tender, but also something sublime, transcendent, and mysterious—something that is distinctly

Other than our poor selves, and that makes us bow in humility of spirit and tremble with a consciousness of awe and adoration. Saint Augustine has put it best in his famous sentence: "I tremble and I thrill. I tremble because I know that I am unlike Him. I thrill because I feel myself like Him." Plotinus has happily hit upon both these essential aspects for religion. God is both beyond and at the same time near. He is transcendent and yet immanent. He is, as Source, above all that can be thought or fathomed, but at the same time, as the overflowing Life of all that is, he is here with us and of us—closer than breathing.

This One, or Source, of Plotinus must not be thought of as an abstract Reality separated from Mind and Soul and considered in its lonely isolation as a pure Blank. As Dean Inge happily puts it, the One is "the transcendence of separability rather than the negation of plurality." He continues: "Without attempting to picture to ourselves the nature of the One, we can understand that as all things participate in unity, in different degrees, and as the path to reality is a progress from lower unities to higher unities, there must be at the top of the ascent an absolute unity, a perfect simplicity, above all differentiation. It is not the weakest and poorest of all numbers, but the plenitude of all and the source of all."[1] It has all the richness and the fullness that get revealed in Mind and Soul, for they are only an overbrimming outflow of its superabundance. Plotinus, it must be remembered, is never applying to ultimate realities our usual categories of quantity. When he is talking about spiritual realities he does not think of them in a framework of time and space. For this reason the word "infinite" is one of the poorest terms we can use, since it has no significance for what is not in space. So, too, if we introduce the word "eternal," we must take care to keep from thinking of it as something that begins after time ceases, or as endless existence going on in time.

"Eternity," Plotinus says (I, 5. 7) "is not a more or less or a thing of any magnitude, but is the unchangeable, the indivisible, timeless Being." Plotinus rejects dry and abstract universals which are empty of con-

---
[1] *The Philosophy of Plotinus*, vol. ii, pp. 108–109.

tent. Realities are not aggregates—they are integral wholes. Change does not proceed from antecedent causes to subsequent effects; we are in the realm of self-activity. He does not predicate attributes to the eternal Source of all that is real. That is too cheap. The One does not possess goodness or beauty or love or truth, for the One *is* Love and Truth and Beauty and Goodness. The world is not "created" or "caused" by the One as though it came "after" his creative act began to operate. All that is truly real in the world around us is an overflow from the One and has its being in the One, as our own thoughts and purposes spring out of what we are.

"On the earth the broken arcs; in the heaven a perfect round."

We see vital things spread out space-wise and proceeding one after the other time-wise. In the One all that is Real is held together, as for us the notes of music are united into a harmony above temporal succession of notes, or as a work of art is held as a single whole in the mind of the artist. All the multitudinous congeries of forms and laws and truths and ideas and goals of reality that make the universe are united at this Apex of creative energy above the division into parts or the differentiation of subject and object. We humans have a preference for thought spread out into the differentiation of subject and object, and we feel lost as we try to contemplate a One that knows no division—a *totum simul,* as the schoolmen called this contemplative state. It is difficult for us to leave atomisms, and mechanisms, and quantities, and separations, and aggregations behind; but if we look within, we shall begin to feel the meaning of a One not made of parts, of a unity that is not compounded, of a fullness that has not come from addition, of a self-activity that is deeper than thinking. The One at the center is absolute unity, complete fullness, the ultimate Source from which all truth and beauty and goodness have flowed out and spread through the world.

The first outflow or overflow, according to Plotinus' system of thought, is called in his Greek phrase *nous,* which might be translated "mind" or, in freer expression, "the world of Spirit." It is what Plato and Kant call "the noumenal universe," that is, the universe of absolute reality. It is the kingdom of creative reason; the realm of eternal thought-forms or ideas or laws or organizing principles. It is the domain of all spiritual values. It is the first stage of emergence or of differentiation. The realm of Mind includes both the divine, creative Thinker and all the forms and patterns of his thought. Plotinus says (V, 1. 4): "*Nous* possesses all things simultaneously. It possesses all things unchanged in identity. It *is;* it knows no past or future; all things in the 'noumenal world' co-exist in an eternal Now." Plato had already explained in the *Timaeus,* that *eternity is God manifesting his own nature.*

It must be remembered that Plotinus is one of the earliest thinkers to formulate a doctrine of the Trinity. He calls *Nous* "a second God," "a first-born Son" who is eternally begotten. Here in this realm of mind there is a subject over against an object—a unity, but a unity in difference. The thought-forms which give our universe its reality, its permanence, its mathematical order, its meaning, its significance, its values, are born from the activity of this world of

Nous, this realm of mind. The mental activity and the thought-forms which are the objects of the activity together constitute *Nous,* so that *Nous* means both Mind and the realm of Ideas which are the objects of Mind. In the *Nous,* Plotinus says (III, 8. 8), "There is complete identity of Knower and known." We must not, however, think of this "world of spirit," this "noumenal universe," as though it were sundered from the One, its Source, and had "gone out" as an independent reality. "Nothing," Plotinus says (V, a.l.), "is completely severed from its prior." It has no more "gone out" than our own mental activity and the objects of our thought "go out" and can be cut apart from *that which we are in our deepest nature.* Plotinus endeavors to make the truth of the situation clear in a figure. A luminous body emits light, he says, without losing any of its substance—the light is an overflow of its inherent nature. Somewhat so the Over-Mind brims over from the superabundant reality of the One. A spiritual kingdom flows or floods out into being and into activity, and yet nothing is lost to the One—the more that is given out the more remains in. Shakespeare has caught the idea in his *Measure for Measure*:

"If our virtues
 Did not go forth of us, 'twere all alike
 As if we had them not."

Here, then, in the divine universe of mind, that issues from the hidden center, are all the forms of thought, all the patterns in the mount, which the world exhibits in such multifarious profusion. As there can be no cathedral without first an architectural plan of it, so there can be no cosmic order, no proportions, or regularities, no predictable certainties, no unvarying laws, no conservation of values, without the realm of Mind and its world of objects where they originate and abide. On this "firm foundation" of eternal Reason the frame of things stands sure and unshaken.

"Thou dost preserve the stars from wrong;
 And the most ancient heavens, through Thee are
  fresh and strong."

And our own minds, so far as we have any, are an organic part of that realm of Over-Mind. We have "come out" into individuation, but we have never broken wholly away from our true "Mother," the world of Mind above us. Our thoughts and experiences correlate with the mighty frame of things precisely because we are at the top of our minds undivided from the kingdom of the Spirit in which we live and move and have our intellectual being. *Nous* is both in our minds and immanent in the world around us—the foundational reality of all that is rational, beautiful, and good.

At the same time this realm of spiritual reality—the *Nous*—like its Source, is in turn superabundant and overbrims with a second overflow of reality which Plotinus calls the *psyche,* and which is usually translated "Soul" or "Oversoul," or it might be named the universal Soul, or perhaps the World-Soul. It is in inseparable connection with the kingdom next above it, penetrated with intelligence and wisdom and the bringer of the Divine down into the lower world where we are denizens though our true citizenship is forever above. The Soul is the principle of creative energy. It is the *élan vital* of the universe. It is life. It is the generative force. It is the urge. It is the guiding power immanent in all things. Its function is like that of the seminal reason, the *logos spermaticos,* of the Stoics. It operates in the world very much as the soul operates in the body. It is the creative life-energy present and active through all process of change and transformation. It lives in and through all organisms. It is the unifying basis, the organizing activity wherever life or organic "wholes" appear. It is the *providence* of the universe, the purposive energy at the heart of things—slumbering and quiescent, even in inorganic nature. The realm, or kingdom, of Soul, then, corresponds to the world of life. It is, as I have said, bound in unbroken unity with the *Nous* that is above it, and whatever it engenders holds, consequently, a measure of Reason in it. "Any object," Plotinus says (III, 2. 16), "in which life is present is at once enreasoned in the sense that the activity peculiar to life is formative, shaping as it moves." It is, he adds, like "the unity or harmony of a drama even though it is torn with struggle."

The Soul is in a sense "amphibious." It can live in two worlds. "Every man is double." He can live upward toward the realm of spirit, or he can live downward toward the world of matter. Here lie both the glory and the tragedy of life. We are "bound by gold chains" to the realm above us and yet we walk down here with feet of clay. We muckrake for straws though a crown is just above our heads. We have infinite wealth hidden within us and, notwithstanding, we may drop to a level hardly above the vegetative scale. But Soul, even at its lowest, carries within itself a "homesickness" for the world above, which is our only home. "There is always a radiance in the inner soul of man, untroubled like the light in a lantern in a wild turmoil of wind and tempest" (I, 4. 7). The individual soul is never wholly sundered from the Oversoul. There is no wall or bar or open space between our souls and the great Mother-Soul in whom we live. "The single soul," Plotinus says (III, 5. 5) "holds to the All-Soul, never cut off, but embraced within it"—hence our "touch of the upward desire." "Each soul," he says, "holds from the divine Soul and is its offspring." In one sense, the truest sense of all, the soul does not "come down." It does not leave its "home." "It exists here," Plotinus says (IV, 2. 2), "and yet is there. It remains in unsundered identity. It is parted and not parted." It never knew any *"coming"* (III, 4. 5). In other words, there is something in us to the very last that "never lets go" of the Source above us—there is something of God in us that keeps the upward attachment alive and gives us "travail pangs" and "birth-pains." The downward slant, or "tilt," as Plotinus calls it, is due to our desire for separateness, our tendency to break away and live on our own, apart from the larger life. We want to be a separate self, an ego-life—somebody on our own account. This striving for isolation is the ground of much of our tragedy and most of our unhappiness. There is something of God present wherever there is mind or soul: that is, wherever there is thought, or love, or creative energy, just as there is something of the sun present wherever there is light, or color or actinic energy. Whenever my mind in flights of fancy sweeps across intervening spaces and visits Egypt, for instance, and contemplates the pyramids, I discover, as soon as I pull myself together, that my mind has not actually *gone* anywhere. It has not left its mooring in my being and journeyed out to foreign parts. It has *stayed here* at least as truly as it has *gone there*. So it is with the Mind and Soul of God. They both "go" and "stay." They are both "out" and "in." Love is the way back to unity and peace.

Plotinus describes the harmonious life in the figure of the performers in a choral dance (III, 6. 2). "They sing together," says he, "though each one has his particular part, and sometimes one voice is heard while the others are silent; and each brings to the chorus something of his own; it is not enough that all lift up their voices together; each must sing choicely his own part to the music set for him." Richard Watson Dixon has put this idea of the soul into some fine lines as follows:

> "There is a Soul above the soul of each,
>   A Mightier Soul which yet to each belongs:
> There is a sound made of all human speech,
>   And numerous as the concourse of all songs:
> And in that Soul lives each, in each that Soul,
>   Tho' all the ages are its lifetime vast;
> Each soul that dies in its most sacred whole
>   Receiveth life that shall forever last."

The world of sense, our world of time and

space down here, is the creative product of the world of mind and the world of soul expressed through the time-process and in the framework of space. In other words, it is reality compounded with matter, whatever *that* is.

Matter appears to be little more than an indefinite intermediate receptacle for form; that is, for the creative energies which have their origin above. "Matter is a certain base, or recipient of Form-Ideas" (II, 4. 1). Plotinus very often talks as though the world of our senses were a reflection of the realm of higher reality seen in the mirror of matter, as one sees his shadow in a stream of running water. There is something there but the reality comes from higher up. "It is from the Divine that all light comes" (II, 4. 5).

Plotinus refines away his "matter" until it seems to become nonexistent, the sheer absence of reality, "the void of all good," "something whose very nature is one long *want*." And yet it is never quite "nothing." It is the factor in the universe that has "no residue of good in it," "the underlying substratum not yet brought to order by the

Ideal-Form." It is "the ever-undefined," "the never at rest," "the all-accepting, but never sated," and so it is the principle and ground of evil. The death of the soul, Plotinus says (I, 8. 10) "is to become sunk in the body, to lie down with matter and be drenched with it." "A soul becomes ugly by something foisted upon it, by sinking itself into the alien, by a fall, a descent into body, into matter" (I, 6. 5). One trouble is that matter—in the form of space and time—separates what should be united, splits up, divides, splashes out or "spills out" (I, 4. 10) into multiplicity that which in its union with the world above can be *real* only in unity. Therefore, the world down here, spread out, and seen piecemeal and in a time-process of before and after, is an "appearance" rather than a true reality—it is a cinematograph "show" rather than a *real event*.

Nevertheless, in spite of its fusion and blend with matter, this world is crammed with beauty and everywhere shows the footsteps of the Divine. "Beauty comes by operation of the creative Soul which is the author of beauty in the world of sense. For the soul, a divine thing, a fragment as it were of the primal beauty, makes beautiful to the fullness of their capacity all things whatsoever that it touches and molds" (I, 6. 6). "Beauty is always a *trace* of the Divine. Whenever the soul sees anything that is kin with the Reality that is above, or any trace of that kinship, it thrills with an immediate delight, takes its own to itself and stirs anew to the sense of its own nature and of all its affinity" (I, 6. 2). One of the finest of Plotinus' many fine passages says: "As it is not for those to speak of the beautiful forms of the material world who have never seen them or known their grace—men born blind, let us suppose—in the same way those must be silent upon the beauty of noble conduct and of learning and all that order who have never cared for such things, nor may those tell of the splendor of virtue who have never known the face of Justice and of Moral-Wisdom, beautiful beyond the beauty of the evening star or the dawn" (I, 6. 4).

Here, then, on these three levels we have the universe as Plotinus apprehends it—(1) the One in its unique wholeness of undifferentiated Reality, (2) the World of Mind and Ideal-Forms, and (3) the World of Soul or creative energy, spraying out in its activity into the multiplicity of space and time and matter. He is, as we have seen, strongly trinitarian in his habit of thought; his disciples still more so; and it may be said that his and their influence on Christian trinitarian formulations can hardly be overestimated.

It remains now to speak of "the way back," the return journey from the circumference to the Center. Here is to be found, of course, the ground of the mysticism of Plotinus. Everything below the highest Center of reality is a falling away, a loss, a drop, a journey away from home into the far country. In spite of the fact that Plotinus does not share the excessive dualisms of his age and has much to say of the beauty that adorns the world of sense, it is, nevertheless, to him a world of "reflections" and "appearances" rather than a world of truth and goodness. The real substance is "yonder."

How do we go back to "the dear fatherland"? (1, 6. 8.) "It is not a journey for feet; the feet bring us only from land to land; nor need you think of coach or ship to carry you. You must close the eyes and call instead upon another vision that is to be waked within you, *a vision which is the birthright of all, but which few use*" (I, 6. 8).

The first step is to withdraw into oneself, to become "self-gathered" in one's inner unity, to return to one's essential and authentic nature, to cultivate "the single eye that sees the mighty Beauty." This noblest vision calls for the sternest and uttermost combat and labor. No sacrifice is too great for it. "For," says our guide in these matters, "not he that has failed of the joy that is in color or in visible forms, not he that has failed of power or of honors or of kingdom has failed, but only he has failed who has failed of This, for whose winning he should renounce kingdoms and command over earth and ocean and sky, if only, spurning the world of sense from beneath his feet, and straining to This, he may *see*" (I, 6. 7).

The exile from the "dear homeland" must first of all discover that he is an exile, that he is far from home, outside his "fatherland," and that his exile is due to his separation, his isolation, to the fact that he lives "down" instead of "up," that he says "No" instead of "Yes." He must "turn about," change from "separateness" to "unity" and become possessed with a passion for home, for the Absolute Good. He must go from the outward to the inward, forsake all that is external, "recollect" himself, recover his soul and unite his being in the Oversoul. In a very beautiful passage (VI, 9. 7) Plotinus says: "God, as Plato said, is not far from each person; rather he is very near to all without their knowing it; they themselves flee him, or more truly they flee themselves. Therefore, they cannot understand Him whom they have fled, nor can they, since they have denied their very selves, find any other, just as a child wandering in delirium does not know his own father." Then, after he has "found" himself, he must rise by thought, by concentration, by intuition, by loyalty to truth, by the flame of love for reality, the beauty of which far transcends the beauty of visible objects, until he finds himself "at home" in the realm of *Nous,* the world of Overmind. He will henceforth be done with mechanistic categories, with space and time and matter, and his "objects" of contemplation will be pure realities in a world that really is.

But mind with its pure objects is not the Apex. The Goal is not yet attained. There is one more journey to be accomplished —not with feet nor by ships nor even by the concentration of thought. The journey ends beyond thought, above the division of subject and object, in a union of like with like, in contact with "the mighty Beauty" that is "the real fatherland." At the very last the seeker becomes what he seeks, the seer becomes what he sees. "He belongs to God and is one with him like two concentric circles; they are one when they coincide; and two only when they are separated" (VI, 9.).

The experience is ineffable and cannot be "explained" to those who have not had the joy of entering.

"Since in the vision there were not two things, but seer and seen were one, if a man could preserve the memory of what he was when he was mingled with the Divine, he would have in himself an image of God. For he was then one with God, and retained no difference, either in relation to himself or to others. Nothing stirred within him, neither anger nor concupiscence, nor even reason or spiritual perception or his own personality, if we may say so. Caught up in an ecstasy, tranquil and alone with God, he enjoyed an imperturbable calm; shut up in his proper essence he inclined not to either side, he *turned not even to himself;* he was in a state of perfect stability; he had become stability itself."[2]

This passage is the source and inspiration of most Western mysticism. This is the sample and pattern account of the great attainment. It would be difficult to select any passage from Greek literature that has influenced Christian life on its higher ranges to the same extent as has Ennead VI, book 9, of Plotinus.

Plotinus is the father of the *via negativa,* the way of "stripping" and of "unknowing," the way of entering the fatherland "naked" and "empty-handed." At the same time we should miss the truth he means to teach if we concluded that this highest moment in the life of the soul were a "blank nothing"

---

[2] VI, 9—Dean Inge's translation. Used by permission of the author.

—sheer absence of content. Just the opposite is the fact. The highest moment of love, of beauty, of music, of sublimity are moments when consciousness no longer differentiates into subject and object, when categories of quantity and description are transcended, and when like knows like in "a spell of grandeur" in what Plotinus calls "life's instantaneous infinite"—"an Eternal Now without jolt or change" (III, 7. 5).

III

MEISTER ECKHART

THE fourteenth century in Europe experienced the greatest wave of mystical religion that has ever appeared in any one period of Christian history, and Meister Eckhart is the towering figure in that unique procession of mystical geniuses. It was a period when the century plant of the Spirit bloomed at its richest. Dante, Petrarch, Boccaccio, Chaucer, Cimabue, Giotto, Richard Rolle, Wyclif, Saint Catherine of Sienna and Duns Scotus are a few of the names in that remarkable constellation of great luminaries. They were not all mystics but they were all luminaries. It was a dawning era, heralding a still greater dawn. There seem to be mysterious "mutation" epochs in history when the old levels of life and thought are suddenly passed and when in a burst of surprise a new one is inaugurated. In many aspects the fourteenth century was dark and sad. It had its Black Death, its Babylonish captivity, its imperial and papal schisms, its interdicts, its peasant uprisings and its interminable wars, but it saw also the creation of the greatest Christian poem of all the ages, the erection of the most perfect bell-tower in the world, the culmination of scholastic ingenuity and subtilty, the birth of religious painting, the dawn of the Renaissance and the highest tidal wave of mystical experience.

Why does the poet come at that particular moment, why does the architectural triumph arrive just then, why does the mystic genius flourish precisely at that date? Who can tell when the hour is ripe, who can explain the curve of human progress? The Spirit seems to blow where and when it listeth. There have been a few persons in human history who have felt the life of God with a vividness and a sense of reality beyond what others ever know or feel, and there have also been a few persons who have possessed a unique power of telling about this experience and what it signifies. In the list of the first type I should put Jesus, Saint Paul, Saint John, Saint Augustine, Saint Bernard, Saint Francis, and George Fox. In the second list I should put Plotinus, Dionysius the Areopagite, Saint Augustine, Dante, Eckhart, Ruysbroeck, Jacob Boehme, Saint Teresa, and Saint John of the Cross, while there are many others who belong in one or the other or in both of these lists. Plotinus, though not a Christian, is the "father" of the long succession and it is impossible to conceive of the march of European mystical thought without this Greek prophet at the head of the line.

Eckhart is, I think, the profoundest interpreter of the experience in the long file of those who followed the Alexandrian "father" of the movement. He was not a systematic thinker like Plotinus, and he was not logically as consistent as the Greek philosopher was. But he was much closer in heart to the rank and file of the people. He spoke in the tongue of the common man. He was humble and tender. His fine sympathetic treatment of Martha, the busy burden-bearer, shows his intimate insight into the daily life of those who listened to him. He was, too, always referring with tenderness and gentleness to the purifying and transforming effect of patient suffering, and he ranks it above ecstasy and exalted visions.

It is a thousand pities that we do not have an autobiography from his pen or some letters which tell "how it went with him." It may quite probably be that we could put him in the first list if we knew the facts and experiences of his life. There are intimations, in the *Sermons and Treatises,* that he, like George Fox, had come up through the flaming sword into the paradise of God, had seen and heard and handled, but there are no first-hand accounts of what happened, "when there was mid-sea and the mighty things." We are left to grope in the dark for details of both the outer and the inner life of the man. It was not a century when men wrote autobiographies, though as an exception Suso did, and no disciple had the skill to pass on to us the story of the great mystic's life. We can see him only far off in the mist—a distant peak showing above impenetrable clouds. He is like a massive bowlder which the glacial drift has left. It is not of our rock or strata. It is torn from another age and habitat, but it at least reveals to us the depth and the carrying power of the movement which brought this bowlder into our fields.

I have twice already tried to spell out the lost story of Eckhart's life and to interpret his thought—once in *Studies in Mystical Religion,* and again in a book entitled *At One With the Invisible,* edited by Professor Sneath, but now that we have Eckhart's *Sermons and Treatises* translated both into English and into modern German, there is something more to say. Before this I have always had to dig him out of his own rugged old high German, and it is a satisfaction to be able to read him in contemporary German and comfortable English. But let no one fondly suppose that he can travel through these four hundred and eighty English pages without some gasping and panting.[1] Eckhart is still Eckhart—a mysterious bowlder which the mystical drift of the centuries has deposited. We can walk around him and see his surface, but who can tell what is far within in the central deeps of the man!

Eckhart was studying in the University of Paris when Dante was setting out, "midway in the path of his life," on his marvelous

---

[1] *Meister Eckhart,* by Franz Pfeiffer, translated with some omissions and additions by C. deB. Evans. London, John M. Walkins.

pilgrimage through the realms where the soul of a man awakens to its eternal destiny and finds what kind of a world it has made for itself. Both men owed an enormous intellectual and spiritual debt to Saint Thomas Aquinas, who finished his earthly life (1274) when they were boys, one in Germany, perhaps fourteen at the time, and the other in Florence, then nine years old. Albertus Magnus, Thomas' master, died in 1280, when Eckhart was about twenty, and probably before he came from his home in Thuringia to study in the famous High School of Cologne, where Dominican priests were trained, but the spirit of this scholar, who, like a world conqueror, was named "Magnus," still pervaded the school. Eckhart showed, as so many other great mystics have done, both the traits of Mary and Martha. He was as strong in practical activity as he was in quiet contemplation. A large part of his life was occupied with the complicated work of administration. He was made prior of the Dominican Convent in Erfurt in 1298 and vicar-provincial of Thuringia. His work in the University of Paris began in 1300 and there two years later he received the degree of Master, and by the title of "Meister" he has ever since been known. He was elected provincial of the Province of Saxony in 1303 and re-elected four years later, with the added task of reforming the convents of Bohemia. When his period of service came to an end in 1311 he gave professional lectures in Paris for three years, after which he taught for a short period in Strasbourg. Then came again three years of administrative work as prior in Frankfort, and finally in 1320 he was made professor of the Dominican School at Cologne, where he remained until his death in 1327.

Eckhart knew the fathers and the masters of mystical theology. They appear and reappear by name in his sermons, are reverently cited as authorities, and even when they are not named their influence can everywhere be seen. He shows also the marked influence of the Arabian Commentators of Aristotle, and the tendency of Arabian scholars toward pantheism is in evidence both in his psychology and in his theology.

Let us stop here for a moment and consider the lines of thought and experience which shaped the mental and spiritual life of this great mystical leader of the thirteenth and fourteenth centuries. He was, we must remember, living in pretty much the same intellectual atmosphere which Thomas Aquinas breathed, and he almost completely spanned the period of the lifetime of the great Florentine poet, who also was a mystic of immense depth and range. These men all read the same books and fed their souls on the same spiritual food. Aristotle had, since the middle of the thirteenth century, become the major intellectual influence, working on men's minds as a mighty leaven. But there was another strand of influence which, if less conscious in their thought, was hardly less profound in their lives. This was the neoplatonic line of thought which came down to them through Saint Augustine on the one hand, and on the other through the great mystic who wrote under the name of "Dionysius," and who claimed to be the convert of Saint Paul on the Areopagus in Athens, when the apostle said, "In God we live and move and are."

In what strange ways human torches are lighted by the Spirit! By what unexpected kindly processes the trail of light goes forward across the centuries! A Carthaginian rhetorician, who had been living an unsettled and wayward life, is converted in a garden at Milan and becomes the greatest pillar of the church after Saint Paul, the Christian channel of neoplatonism and the father of Western theology and of Western mysticism. An anonymous Greek scholar, living perhaps in Edessa at the end of the fifth century, turns the system of Plotinus and his followers into an elaborate form of Christian mysticism and transmits it to the gifted minds of the thirteenth and fourteenth centuries.

In the Seventh Book of his *Confessions* Saint Augustine tells us that a Latin translation of certain neoplatonist books—evidently the works of Plotinus—came into his hands in 385 and proved to be one of the most potent influences in preparing the way for his conversion to Christianity. It was here in these books that the young Augustine discovered that the inner eye of the soul is able to see the Eternal Light from which the soul itself has sprung, and he learned for the first time that the Platonists agreed with Saint John in teaching that the Word was with God and that the Word was God. It was again, he says, the books of the Platonists that admonished him to "enter into my inmost self" to find God, and when he sets forth his later attainment of that great goal, it is given in neoplatonic language: "In one trembling flash above the mind I arrived at *That which Is.*" In the sublime experience at Ostia, with his mother by his side, he says, "We came to our own minds, and then passed beyond them . . . with the utmost leap of our hearts. . . . We reached forth and with one flash of thought touched the Eternal Wisdom that abides over all." These famous passages, and that other word of his: "Thou hast made us for thyself, and our hearts are restless until they rest in thee," were to be the guiding light of all later mystics to be formed in the Western Church.

Even more important was the influence of "Dionysius," since he presented, as Saint Augustine did not, a complete and systematized account of the mystic way. He furnished the terms and the vocabulary. He produced in ready-made form the philosophy which became the working basis for all mystics before the Reformation. He accustomed everybody to think of God as absolutely above and beyond all description in terms of qualities and character—a God who is super-everything, and who is to be "known" only through an experience that transcends "knowing." In the middle of the ninth century the Irish scholar, John Scotus Erigena, translated these books of "Dionysius" from Greek to Latin and put them into current thought. They were, of course, given great prestige by the fact that they were believed to be written by the man whom Saint Paul had converted on Mars' Hill who was believed to be the first Bishop of Athens and to be also Saint Denis, the founder of Christianity in Paris, and who finally became, as they supposed, a holy martyr to the faith.

Through these two sources, then, the streams of mystical life and thought flowed into and became a part of European Christianity. Gregory the Great, who was Pope from 590 to 604, and Saint Bernard of Clairvaux (1090-1153), one of the greatest spiritual personalities in the entire history of the church, became powerful transmitters of the mystical inheritance. Saint Bernard gave to it a new note of warmth and passionate love, and he added to mystical literature the glowing and vivid imagery of the *Canticles*, turned into a pictorial drama of the soul wedded to its eternal Bridegroom. The two great Victorines—Hugh and Richard of Saint Victor in Paris—in the twelfth century raised the method of *contemplation* to a place of immense importance, and carried the mystical tradition a new stage forward. In England, Richard Rolle (born c. 1290), one of the earliest English poets, the father of English prose, and a "troubadour of God," was the first great English mystic. Rolle was followed in the middle of the fourteenth century by a great anonymous spiritual genius who translated parts of the writings of "Dionysius" into English and who produced an extraordinary book entitled *A Cloud of Unknowing* which ends with these words of hope: "Not what thou art, nor what thou hast been, seeth God with his merciful eyes, *but what thou wouldst be.*" We may think of Meister Eckhart, then, as the person who gathers up all these streams of mystical life and thought, and who in a very real sense, therefore may be said to be the culmination of neoplatonized Christian mysticism.

Eckhart was a man of books before he became an administrator and a popular preacher, and with all his genius and originality he still carries a large cargo of thought derived from his predecessors and forerunners, which is equally true, of course, of Dante. I often wonder as I am slowly, patiently creeping along through these sermons of Eckhart, what would happen if he could appear among us again and preach his messages to a modern audience! They would be too deep for any congregation that assembles anywhere now—even in our colleges and universities or theological seminaries. It would seem to us food for giraffes, not for lambs, and yet the common people heard him gladly and the multitude crowded in when he preached, as he usually did, in the vernacular speech, and, fortunately, his words were sacredly preserved for coming generations. Mysticism was in the atmosphere then and Eckhart talked in the style and language of his time. We have lost the key both to his phraseology and to the experiences which lay behind his words. We had, however, better not assume too hastily that we have got beyond the stars by which he sailed, or that our modern education has enabled us to reach depths of life and thought unknown to him six hundred years ago.

Two years after Eckhart's death, which occurred, as I have said, in 1327, a papal Bull condemned twenty-eight propositions drawn from his writings. Seventeen of these were pronounced "heretical" and the other eleven were called "ill sounding, rash, and suspect." The Bull declares that "he wished to know more than he should"! There can be no question that "he wished to know" more than the formulated doctrines which the church proclaimed, more than the official authorities could tell him, more than priests or bishops or Popes of the period were able to see. He has his spiritual daughter, "Sister Katrei," say that she cannot find eternal life until she goes on beyond the teaching of the church and beyond the best guidance her confessor can give her and severs all ties with "creatures," that is, human helpers, and puts herself "in the mighty hands of God."

"I am sorry," she says, "that I listened so long to the counsels of men and was deaf to the counsel of the Holy Spirit." This marvelous story of *Sister Katrei* may, I think, be taken as the nearest approach we have to an autobiographical document, and we can, I believe, find revealed in it the steps and stages of the soul's journey upward to God —"the Source from whence the soul flowed forth." But Eckhart was, notwithstanding, a loyal member of the church. He never intended to break with the system that had nurtured him. He had no thought of being a "rebel" or a "heretic." He could hardly have conceived of a great spiritual life going on without the ministration and the means of grace which the church supplied. The nearest he approached to the attitude of the Reformation can be seen in a passage like the following: "As for those who see their salvation in outward practices [what Luther called "works"] I do not say they will be lost, but they will get to God only through hot cleansing fires; for they who do not quit themselves follow not God; keeping hold of themselves they follow their own darkness. God is no more to be found in any bodily exercise than He is to be found in sin. . . . The beginning of the holy life is to be found in the work of the inner man, in vision and in loving."[2]

Eckhart is a true and characteristic "Friend of God" of the fourteenth-century type. He belonged to the church. He loved its sacraments, he accepted its august system, and he was enrolled in its hierarchy, but at the same time he insisted upon the inalienable right of the individual soul to find its own direct pathway to God, and he stoutly maintained that "the school of the Holy Spirit is the highest school of all," in which "a person can learn more in the twinkling of an eye than all the doctors can teach him."[3] "Not all the saints in heaven," he says, "nor all the preaching friars and barefoot monks on earth can stand against one man moved by the truth."[4]

It is among the fragments and sayings of Eckhart that we find the charming story of "a learned doctor" who yearned for some one to instruct him in the way of truth. Finding one day a beggar, his feet all

---
[2] Tractate on *The Kingdom of God*.
[3] *Sister Katrei*.
[4] *Ibid.*

cracked and dirty, his body clothed in rags, he said to the beggar, "God give thee a good day."

"I never had a bad one," said the beggar.

"God give thee good fortune."

The beggar replied, "I never have bad fortune."

"God bless thee."

Said the beggar, "I have never been accursed."

When he is asked what he means by this excessive optimism the beggar explains thus: "Thou dost wish me a good day and I say I never had a bad one. Hungry, I praise God; freezing, I praise God; poor and forsaken withal, I praise God, so I never have a bad day. Thou dost wish me good fortune; I say I never have ill fortune. Whatever God gives or may lay up for me, be it sour or sweet, good or bad, I accept all from God for the best, and so I have no ill hap. Thou dost call down God's blessing upon me. I answer I am not accursed. I have given my will up to God, every whit, so that anything that God wills I will. That is why I am never unblessed."

"Yea," said the doctor, "but suppose God

should choose to cast thee into hell, what wouldst thou say to that?"

"Cast me into hell," said the beggar. "That would spite himself, yet *if* he cast me into hell I should still have two arms to clasp him with. One arm is true humility, and this I should put under him, embracing him all the while with the other arm, which is love. *Better to be in hell with God than in heaven without him.*"[5]

This shows emphatically how far Eckhart and his "Friends of God" have traveled beyond the external and traditional Christianity of their time. Heaven and hell for him, as for Dante, are to be found in the inward state and attitude of the soul. You will be eternally what you are in your deepest inner self. No jugglery will change it; no masses or pilgrimages can alter the eternal moral conditions of life. You must some day meet your naked self, *and it will be what it is*—and that will be heaven or hell. He says boldly: "Theologians speak of hell. I will tell you what hell is. Your state here is your eternal state. This *is* hell or heaven." "Each per-

---

[5] Whittier has attributed this incident to John Tauler of Strasbourg and he has beautifully told it in his poem, "Tauler."

son," he adds, "will be his own judge in this sense, namely, that the state he then appears in [at death] he will be in eternally."[6]

Eckhart, like all great prophets of the spiritual life, is forever done with schemes of barter and double-entry bookkeeping. His "Sister Katrei" says: "Though there were neither hell nor heaven, I would follow God for true love all the same. I would follow him to the end, without a 'why' [that is, without calculation], or other reason than himself." He goes the whole way out on the road where the milestones are not counted. *Love,* for him, must be washed clean of all self-seeking, of all thought of a return. "To be able to say, 'I love thee, Lord,' a person must suffer without why that which without why Christ suffered, and he must suffer it joyously and gladly. Though God should tell him mouth to mouth, 'Thou shalt be lost forever with the damned,' he only loves God all the more, and says, 'Lord, as thou wilt that I be damned, damned I will be eternally.' That person can truly say to God, 'I love thee.'" It is a relief to our modern minds that Eckhart was absolutely sure to

---
[6] *Sister Katrei.*

begin with that God could not, from his very moral nature, damn a soul that did not deserve to be damned; for, after all, hell consists only in being *eternally what you are.*

"Art thou looking for God," he asks in the Sermon numbered XI, "seeking God with a view to thy own personal good, thy personal profit? Then in truth thou art not seeking *God.*" He cites a philosopher who says, "He who has once been touched by truth, by righteousness, by goodness, though it entailed the pangs of hell, that man could never turn therefrom, not for an instant," and he adds his own conclusion: "The man who is moved by truth, righteousness, and goodness can no more quit these three things than God can quit his Godhead." In his fortieth Sermon he declares: "If thou seekest aught of thine own, thou wilt never find God, for thou art not seeking God merely. Thou art seeking something with God, making a candle of God, as it were, with which to find something, and then having found it, throwing the candle away." There are plenty of persons, he says in another Sermon, the twelfth, "who follow our Lord half way, but not the other half." Eckhart's peculiarity consisted in going "the whole way" to the very end.

There is a story out of this same fourteenth century which tells how an old woman was seen one day in the streets of Strasbourg carrying a torch in one hand and a bucket of water in the other. When she was asked what her strange performance signified, she said that with the torch she was going to burn up heaven and with the bucket of water she was going to put out hell fire, so that henceforth men could be good for the mere love of God and of goodness and not for the sake of results in the unseen world. She had no doubt heard Eckhart preach and was giving a vivid pictorial illustration of his frequent theme.

The central note in Eckhart's Sermons, and his most important contribution to mystical thought, is his profound interpretation of the nature of the soul. "God made man's soul so like himself," he says in the sixth Sermon, "that nothing else in heaven or earth resembles God so closely as does the human soul." "To measure the soul," he says in his *Sister Katrei,* "you must gauge it with God, for the ground of God and the ground of the soul are one nature." "When I saw into myself," he says in the same tractate, "I saw God in me and everything God ever made in earth and heaven." The truth is to be found not outside, it is within, wholly within. "Ye men, why do ye look without for that which is within you?"

But the truth is not in the surface-mind; it is deep down in the ground and innermost center of the soul, as subsoil wealth. This innermost core of our being Eckhart calls by many different names, such as "Fünklein" or "Spark," "Apex of the Soul," "Centre," "Ground," "Synteresis," "Innermost Essence," "Inner Light," "Bottomless Abyss," "The Arcanum of the Mind"; but however he names it, he is always maintaining that there is something in the soul that is unsundered from God and that indivisibly attaches to the divine nature. This exalted doctrine of the soul is, of course, not new with Eckhart. His forerunners had already held that man's soul is not from the realm of matter nor from the world of space. It is at its highest point of the same nature as God. Aristotle taught that the active creative reason in man can have no earthly origin, while Plotinus went even further and talked of mind and soul as emanations of God, but they are emanations that in going out never actually *leave* their source, as our ideas are still ours however much we utter them. There is an apex or center within us that can never let go and break away from its divine life and spiritual fount. It is because Eckhart believes that there is a junction of the soul with God in the inner deeps of the soul that he can so emphatically declare that "nothing is so close to us as God."

"God is nearer to me than I am to myself."[7] "Thou need not seek Him here or there, He is no further off than the door of thy heart."[8] "In her superior powers the soul is in contact with God."[9] "No man ever wanted anything so much as God wants to make man's soul aware of Himself. God is always ready, but we are far from Him. God is in, we are out; God is at home, we are away somewhere."[10] "When the soul enters into her Ground, into the innermost center of her being, divine power suddenly

---

[7] Sermon LXIX, C. deB. Evans, p. 171.
[8] Sermon IV.
[9] Sermon LII.
[10] Sermon LXIX.

pours into her."[11] "In the Spark, or center of the soul, there occurs true union between the soul and God."[12] "When I saw into myself I saw God in me."[13] "If the soul knew herself, she would know all things."[14] "Where God is there is the soul, and where the soul is there is God."[15]

These random quotations from Eckhart are sufficient to show how bold and daring this fourteenth-century preacher could be. There is something in us, he insists, which has never left its fontal Source and Origin. Travel as far as we may into the world of change and mutability, what he calls "this coil of nether things," we nevertheless remain always at one point in contact with the eternal being of God. There is something which does not let go of him or sever from him, in all the surgings, the ebbs and flows of our temporal life. It is as though in all the mazes of our earthly wanderings we always have hold of an Ariadne thread which connects us with our Guide, a thread that quivers and pulls with all the life and love of God. We are, at the center or Apex of

---

[11] Sermon LXXI.
[12] Sermon LXXIX.
[13] *Sister Katrei.*
[14] Sermon X.
[15] Sermon LXXXIII.

our soul, joined in essence with him, as spirit with Spirit.

"Why do ye ever go out?" he cries. "Why not stop at home and mind your own treasure? For indeed the whole truth is native in you."[16] It is always possible to withdraw from temporal things, from our busy activities and hot pursuits, and to *center down* into this unlost divine inheritance within us. We are suddenly *at home*. We have entered That which Is—the changeless and eternal. We have come upon the primal Source. We are beyond the distinctions of time and place, healed of the wounds that come from our private preferences, by the plunge into the living unity of the Godhead. The floodgate which takes us into the silent refuge where God repairs these broken vessels of ours is close at hand within our own selves.

It is, however, not enough to sink down into the deeps of the soul, to leave the noises of the world behind, and to enter into the stillness of the Godhead. Man's supreme business here on earth is to let God give birth to his own nature in the soul, or, as Eckhart

---
[16] Sermon XIII.

usually puts it, to let God bring forth his Son in the soul. God in his deepest nature as the Ground and Source of all reality is called by Eckhart the Godhead. As naked Godhead he is utterly beyond our comprehension. But as he comes forth out of his hidden and ineffable being into revelation and expression he is then God made manifest. The most perfect manifestation of God is to be seen in Christ, who is by nature what God himself is. But not once only does God bring forth his Son. Every soul is susceptible to this birth of God, and God strives in every one of his human creatures to accomplish this marvelous event. "The best thing God ever did for man," Eckhart says, "was to become man himself," and the highest moment in any man's life is that moment when the divine nature as a spiritual seed becomes the active, dominating principle in the man. Then the "old man" is transformed into a "new man." This is for Eckhart a mystical event of the highest order. When God has brought forth his Son in a man there arises in the soul a love-spring, a joy like the joy of birds. There is a welling-in of life and power. There is a burst of exuberant spirit. Not only the deep ground of the soul now partakes of God and shares in his being, but the whole human nature of the man is shot through with the light and love of God—the man becomes by grace what Christ was by nature. God is essentially spiritualized being, and when God brings forth his Son in us we too by his life in us become at length spiritual beings in our new-found nature.

The most baffling thing to deal with among the problems of life and thought is the real meaning of *time* and *space*. Do they belong to the ultimate nature of the universe or are they caused by our manner of perceiving? Are they truly real or are they only specious? Are they facts of reality or are they facts only of appearance? Do they pertain to the deepest essence of things or only to the surface accidents? Eckhart's answer is closely allied to the ancient Platonic one —he calls Plato "that great priest who occupied himself with lofty matters." He holds space and time to belong only to the world that is cast as a shadow of the real one—the world of appearance which is like a reflected image in a mirror. "If my face were eternal," he says in Sermon XXXIX, "and were held before a mirror, the face would be received in the mirror as a temporal thing, albeit eternal in itself." "God," he says in the eleventh Sermon, "is *truth, but things in time are not truth.*" It is so with everything that appears to our senses —an eternal reality is splashed out into space and time, and so changed to "appearance." All that is real and true for Eckhart is time-free and space-free. It is not in process; it Is. It does not change; it Abides. It has no before and after; it is an eternal Now. He is adhering to a very ancient and honorable system of thought. He is merely reaffirming the well-known tradition that what is perfect cannot change into something else, for then it would become either more perfect or less perfect; consequently he sees no way to insure perfection except to think of it as belonging in a sphere above our kind of world where events proceed from before to after.

Any description of his "eternal Now" is bound to be marked with inconsistency, because we men with our time goggles on are always prone to think of this "eternal Now" as *an infinitely long stretch* in which "nothing happens"—an endless quiescence. That is entirely to miss Eckhart's meaning. What he is endeavoring to say is that all that is true and real, beautiful and good in the entire universe is held together in an undivided unity as one living whole, somewhat as a musician holds the multitudinous notes of his symphony in one unbroken melody which transcends the successive time-notes. Eckhart's moments of mystical experience seem to bring him into a state so exalted and so completely time-free that he interprets the whole life of God in terms of it—a moment like *that* seems to him to have the richness of "an eternal Now."

God and the soul are, in Eckhart's way of thinking, not in space or time—they belong to what is intrinsically, or essentially, *real*. "If," he says, "the soul were stripped of all her sheaths, God would be discovered all naked to her view and would give himself to her, withholding nothing. As long as the soul has not thrown off all her veils, however thin, she is unable to see God."[17] The Apex of the soul, the *Fünklein,* is a timeless, an

---

[17] Sermon XLII.

eternal reality. "At its summit the soul has no connection with time."[18] "There is one loftiest part of the soul," he says, "which stands above time and knows nothing of time or of body," that is, of things in space.[19] "At the summit of the soul time has never entered and no form was ever seen at the summit of the soul."[20] Again he says, "There is a power in the soul untouched by time and flesh, flowing from the Spirit, remaining in the Spirit, altogether spiritual. In this power is God, ever verdant, flowering in all the joy and glory of the actual self."[21] When we "rise past our own mind to the summit of mind," from this divine eminence we have "an inkling of the perfection and stability of eternity, for there is neither time nor space, neither before nor after, but everything present in one new fresh-springing *now*, where millenniums last no longer than the twinkling of an eye!"[22] "I have often said," he declares, "that God is creating the whole world now this instant."[23] Eternity is not something before time began or after time shall be over. Eternity is *a timeless now*, in which God and

---

[18] Sermon XCV.
[19] Sermon XI.
[20] Sermon LXVI.
[21] Sermon VIII.
[22] Sermon XII.
[23] Sermon LXVI.

the soul have no need for clocks or calendars, nor for rapid transit from place to place. "Time ends," says Eckhart, "where there is no before and after."[24] Everything that *is* is now and here for the spirit that partakes of God, for the soul in whom the divine birth has occurred.

> "Alles vergängliche
> Ist nur ein Gleichniss,"

Goethe wrote at the end of *Faust*. "Everything transitory is only a symbol or parable." That is what the Platonists and their disciples, the mediæval mystics, are always saying. The real world is not in space and time—it is a super-temporal, a super-spatial reality. The trouble with this exalted view is that it at once makes everything real and eternal absolutely unknowable for us who live in time and a *sheer blank* for our human observation and thought. Eckhart, of course, knows that as well as any critic does—he knows it and he glories in it. God, that is, the God-head, the ultimately Real, for him is "the nameless Nothing," "the empty Desert where no one is at home."

[24] Sermon XCIV.

God, he says, and likewise the soul born of God, is "beyond time, in eternity above images," "above multiplicity." He is "essence," not "accident"—"pure unadulterated being." We cannot know what God is; "we can only know what he is not." "The mind must be raised to an *unknowing knowing*." "Where creature stops, God begins." "Enter God, exit creatures." "To know God is to know him as unknowable."

These are surely hard sayings. They are not only "hard" for the simple lowly lambs; they are "hard" also for the giraffes with their high heads. Something is wrong when the solution of a problem is more difficult to understand than the problem itself! We have left our type of rationality behind when we begin to talk of "unknowing knowing," and when we relegate the supreme reality of our universe to the blank of "a nameless Nothing," to "the empty stillness of absolute Naught." This is only another way of saying that the problem of life, of thought, of religion, like the problem of the relation between the circumference and diameter of a circle, is insoluble in terms of our mind, and that our best gesture under the circumstances is to put the hand upon the mouth! If space and time are unreal, and everything the mind can deal with is only "appearance," and if God and the essence of the soul belong to an order of being to which space and time do not in any sense attach, then, of course, Eckhart is right and about both these supreme realities we can say nothing, know nothing, think nothing. We must, as he says, "turn to *unknowing* to find them."

I am, however, not ready yet for his alternative. It lands him in the deepest, darkest agnosticism and nescience. It writes "mene" on the whole visible frame of things. Evermore we come out by the same door as in we went. We arrive nowhere. It makes the incarnation an unreality. It nullifies the significance of moral struggle. It turns evolution and historical progress into an empty dream. It lands us in a chaos of *maya* and illusion. There is nothing stable for our feet to stand upon. The Holy Grail itself becomes dust and ashes. Eckhart consistently turns the gospel story into a subtle allegory. Everything Christ said and did stands in his mind for some remote and hidden reality. The miracles and parables point to timeless truth. When we turn to Eckhart's sermon on the son of the widow of Nain, we find that the widow stands for the soul. Her son represents the intellect, and we are whirled away from the event at Nain to something beyond space and time. Nothing is what it obviously and naturally *seems* to be. Eckhart is doing no more than any other scholar of his time in his farfetched use of allegory. It was an obsession all the way down from Philo to the Reformation, and it blinded all eyes to the simple glory and beauty and truth of the gospel story.

But it is impossible legitimately to pass by allegory from a world where events happen, a world of joy and sorrow, a world of moral and spiritual issues, to a world where time and space, before and after, have ceased to exist. We are left gazing at a blank. We change our rich, colorful world for a pure abstraction. Our human vocabulary loses all its meaning. We are in very truth in "a desert where no one is at home." Nothing in this world of ours is a bit like that world of infinite immobility and absolute immutability. Our figures all fail, our allegories all miss the mark, our similes are futile. There is a chasm between the two worlds which nothing can bridge, not even imagination. Nothing we know, or can know, under this system of thought throws the least light upon the nature of the world yonder. God as he is revealed to us in time and space is wholly unlike the Godhead who remains for us hidden, changeless, unknowable, of whom we can only say: "Not! Not! Not this! Not that! Not here! Not there!" There is no hope in Christianity, nor in any form of religious faith, if we must go to the needy world of our time and say to men who are in quest of light and relief that God is an unknown timeless Center of quiescence, shut up in the tranquillity of his own inner being, never to be known or found here in our vale of mutability, where birth and death, and love and hate, smiling and weeping are real events for us.

Eckhart is not to blame for this impasse. It was not quite so sharply put by his forerunners. But he found it and he left it. He went round and round this sheer rock which no man had ever climbed, and he left it standing there in "a mist of unknowing." This "negative" philosophy is no proper or inherent part of mysticism. It belongs to a long and tragic stage of human thinking. I do not want to do anything to perpetuate it. I want to transcend its abstract reality by substituting for it a reality that is self-communicative and concrete. Instead of being a God whose glory consists in hiding himself in solitary detachment in the desert where nothing stirs, God finds himself in the stress and strain of world-building, in the web and tissue of the moral and spiritual victories of history, of art and of religion, in the slow tragic redemptive work of the ages. He is of such a nature that he can be truly revealed in the events of space and time and history. He is a being, not of abstractness and negations, but of character and purpose.

He is not unknown and unknowable—an inscrutable X—but a God who can make his character known in the love and friendship and sacrifice of Christ, and in our own loyalties and fellowships and moral strivings —a Spirit living in and working with our finite human spirits. To find him we are not compelled to resort to an ecstatic flight into a state in which all the conditions of human existence cease to operate, and from which we can bring back no garnered fruit for use in our hard temporal present. We can find him as a vital healing Presence in the hush and quiet within the deeps of our own souls, and we can find him too wherever we valiantly take up the tasks and duties which spring out of our corporate human relationships. If we are to maintain a triumphant mystical faith to-day, it must fit some such philosophical outlook as that. What Milton said about "cloistered virtue," I should say about a hidden, retired, withdrawn and abstract God: "I cannot praise a fugitive and cloistered virtue, unexercised and unbreathed, that never sallies out and sees her adversary, but slinks out of the race, where that immortal garland is to be run for, not without dust and heat!"

Time and space are, I believe, not unreal. They are not dim shadows of appearance. They are not reflections in a mirror. They have their basis of truth and reality in the essential nature of a spiritual universe. Instead of endeavoring to eliminate them as something foreign and defective, we need, rather, to rise through them to those experiences and insights of unity and wholeness in which we see the meaning of the process and the significance of the struggle in a time-span which holds past, present and future together in a significant *now*. Perhaps God's time-span is an eternal Now in which the entire world-process has its meaning revealed and its justification affirmed. What a moment that would be!

If I cannot indorse and praise Eckhart's abstract and negative philosophy, I can, nevertheless, greatly commend his beautiful spirit and his effective practical faith which towered above his theoretic philosophy and triumphed in spite of his agnostic creed. He had struggled manfully with the most baffling questions of life, he was utterly free from hypocrisy and completely honest with all men and with himself, and without knowing how he did it, he somehow scaled the rock and found himself "close upon the shining tablelands to which our God himself is moon and sun." His contemporaries said that "God hid nothing from Meister Eckhart," and I feel as I read his Sermons, stocked though they are with bad philosophy and worse allegory, that something divine and holy keeps breaking through them. His hearers did not altogether understand him, but they felt an unusual spiritual energy and power coming through *his God-receptive* life. He knew the might of humility and meekness. "Even God," he says, "cannot thwart the humble soul that has towering aspiration." "I would stake my life," he says, "upon the fact that by strength of will a man can pierce a wall of steel."

He is a rare interpreter of love and it is not love in the abstract—it is love that proves itself by loving. Take this fine sentence: "What I thank God most for is for not being able of his greatness to leave off loving me."[25] That broke out of his own deep experience and it makes us know that for him the love of God is no abstraction above space and time, but a warm and tender fact of life. "I have said many times and say again," he declares in his twenty-eighth Sermon, "that *everything our Lord has ever done he did simply to the end that God might be with us and that we might be one with him, and that is the reason why God was made man.*" "The best thing God ever did for man," as I have already quoted, "was to become man

---

[25] Sermon LXXIII.

himself." With all his emphasis on "detachment," "contemplation," withdrawal from the outside to the inside, he nevertheless declares that "it is better to feed the hungry than to spend one's time in contemplation."[26] And he has much to say in favor of busy Martha, who provides the food necessary for life. Again and again he quotes Saint Augustine's phrase, *"The soul is where it loves."* It is the love-spring arising in the soul which bears it back to God.[27]

With love comes suffering, and Eckhart is an expert in the meaning of suffering. In one of his most noted sayings he declares, "A life of rest and peace in God is good; a life of pain in patience is still better; but to have peace in the midst of a life of pain is best of all."[28] "Nothing," he says in his great sermon on suffering, the hundred and fourth, "makes a man so like God as suffering." "I say that next to God there is no nobler thing than suffering. . . . If anything were nobler than suffering, God would have saved mankind therewith."

Our theories and speculations are frail

---
[26] Sermon CI.
[27] Second Tractate.
[28] Sermon LXIX.

and transitory. They cost much sweat and blood and they are precious to *us* as the offspring of our brain, but the heart reaches further and its fruit is much more permanent. When all the chaff of mediæval speculation is winnowed away from these sermons of the great Dominican preacher, the inner spiritual kernel remains as sound and nourishing as when the people crowded in to hear his bold words in their own tongue.

IV

THE INFLUENCE OF THE MYSTICS ON MARTIN LUTHER

ONCE in a long run of years there comes in the historical process a person whose life and character seem in retrospect to have reached an ideal height. Seldom, however, is it possible to point to any co-operative group-event of history which in like degree satisfies our minds. Very rarely indeed do we find any historical achievement which involves the massed contribution of many minds and many hands, that comes up to our ideal of *what ought to have happened*. This failure of an historical event to attain an ideal height is peculiarly true of the Reformation of the church in the sixteenth century. Many reasons can be assigned to explain why the highest human hopes that were surging in men's minds in this great period were not realized. Something certainly went awry, but perhaps as much constructive gain emerged as the epoch was ripe at the time to produce. The dead hand of the past was too heavy to allow the awakened leaders of the Reformation to go all the way through to the goal which they saw in their highest moments of vision. They found it necessary to compromise and adjust at many points in order to hold their forces together and to win over the timid and the conservative to any kind of advance movement. And, as usually happens, the extreme radicals of the period startled everybody with glimpses of the dangers involved in a break with the ancient basis of authority.

What was needed most was a sound formulation of an inward basis of authority in religion to take the place of the waning authority of the external church. But nobody knew how to do it successfully, and gradually the main line Reformers settled down upon another type of external authority. Luther was plainly moving in 1520 toward an inward basis of authority, but he had not brought his difficult problem to a satisfactory solution when a successive series of critical events hurried him on faster than he was prepared to go. His thinking was not matured enough for the crisis. He had not had time to consider and test out ways of constructing a church of the spiritual fellowship type of which he had in high moments pretty clear intimations. If he could have had a few years more of quiet meditation and leisured thinking, he might have found a new and unique way forward, but all of a sudden he was plunged into a whirling vortex, and he had to follow second best lines rather than ideal best ones. I propose to show in this lecture that the mystics had been giving him a very definite insight into the nature of inward religion and were furnishing him with a clue to a deeper way of life than that of external and forensic methods. Events, however, drove him on before the guiding threads were in his hand and before his steps forward could be carefully planned and matured.

It has long been known by all students of Luther's life and thought that at some period of his development he was attracted to the sermons of John Tauler and to the little anonymous mystical book called *German Theology,* but it is only in more recent times that scholars have come to realize the full scope and significance of the influence of the writings of the mystics on the formation of the inner life of the great reformer. I propose in this chapter to trace with some care the lines of that influence and the depth of its impact.

Luther has held a central place in the historical debates of the world for over four hundred years, and there is no noticeable diminution of interest in the problems that gather about his name. Every fleck of light which can be thrown upon his life should be welcome, for, after all the centuries of research, there are still large areas of darkness and mystery remaining. He has always been, and is bound to be, a storm center, a battle figure. He had a persistent habit himself of tangling up the threads of his destiny, and the controversies that have risen over the issues of his life and thought have added a great deal to the tangle. We are now able, I believe, to establish beyond debate or controversy that his study of the mystics marks the turning point of his life and actually swung him from the straight path of a mediæval monk to the incalculable curve of a dynamic reformer. It may, I think, be taken as settled now that the great transforming vision, which altered the whole course of his life, did not come to Luther on the holy staircase in the Lateran at Rome in 1510. That is a tradition which hangs on a slender thread and a very large amount of solid biographical facts makes it quite untenable. He positively says himself, "When I was made a Doctor," which was in October, 1512, "I did not yet know the light." There was a moment when the sudden flash came, when a new insight broke over him, but it came considerably later than 1510 and there had been a long preparation for it, as there always is for visions that are constructive. It was, as I propose to show, the mystics who, in large measure, did this preparatory work on his mind—and inaugurated the new curve. The first stage of his serious contact with mysticism was through one of the great springs and sources of it, namely, in the writings of Saint Augustine, which he began to study about the year 1508. Before that point in his life was reached his main intellectual influence had been the writings of William of Occam and Occam's distinguished disciples, d'Ailly, who was Cardinal of Cambrai, and Gabriel Biel, a professor in the University of Tübingen. They were late

Schoolmen, leaders of so-called Nominalism. They were strongly impregnated with humanism in its early stages, and strongly inclined to exalt man's native capacities and fundamental powers. Luther frequently identifies these "modernist" Schoolmen with scholasticism proper, and when later he revolted from these teachers, that revolt carried with it a rejection in theory of all mediæval scholasticism. He says at a later time that he had "formerly learned among the monstrous things which are almost accounted axioms of scholastic theology" that "man can do his part in acquiring Grace"; that he "can remove obstacles to Grace"; that he "has freedom of choice" and that "his will is able to love God above all things through its purely natural powers."[1] In his later life he brings Schoolmen and their great forerunners under one sweeping indictment and with his usual vigor dubs them all together "hog theologians."

It goes without saying that Luther would have led no reform if he had remained as he was up to 1508, a disciple of Occam and his humanistic followers. He might in that

[1] *Luther's Works*, Weimar Ed., II, p. 401.

case have slowly developed in the direction of Erasmus, but he would not have been a world-shaker. He was awakened from his humanistic "slumber" by the deeper message of the mystics. At first it was, as I have said, the great Carthaginian, Saint Augustine, who set him on a different path and whose writings Luther declared that he "devoured rather than read." The first effect of Augustine's influence on him appears in Luther's *Commentary on the Psalms,* which was written between the years 1513 and 1515, though we also possess his enthusiastic and revealing notes written still earlier on the margin of the works of Saint Augustine, jotted down as he read. He is not yet shaken free from his humanistic outlook. He still believed at this time that salvation was in a man's own hands; there is a certain area of individual freedom; a man can at least prepare himself for the work of Divine Grace. He speaks approvingly of that precious remnant of goodness in the soul which survived the Fall—the inner Spark, or *Synteresis,* as Eckhart and many earlier mystics called the apex of the soul.

But he takes a darker and more pessimistic

view of human life than he formerly had done, and he owes many characteristic expressions and phrases to Augustine, whose influence is much in evidence. It is not primarily the mysticism of Augustine that has been working within him—it is his theology; but at the same time he feels strongly now the appeal of inward, first-hand religion. He is disillusioned over dry dead logic and scholastic debates, and he shows a passion for some direct way to God. His sermons too in 1515 reveal a similar new intensity and depth. The direct personal influence of John von Staupitz at that time was an important factor. Staupitz was in a mild way a mystic, an enthusiastic lover of Bernard of Clairvaux, and he was a wise, affectionate, and intimate friend of Luther in his convent days. John Lang, of Erfurt, was another adviser and helper, who loved the mystics and who helped Luther to discover them. Bernard of Clairvaux became in this period one of his favorite writers. He found in him another spiritual helper. Meditation was the business of a monk, and he thus did not need to go to the great twelfth-century mystic and preacher to learn the importance of inward retreat. What he did learn from Bernard was the necessity of becoming a glowing *lover* of God. The main difficulty with him at this time was that fear rather than love still ruled him. He was afraid of God. He thought of him as arbitrary, a despot, an avenger, a merciless and angry judge. He tells how he longed to understand the apostle Paul, but he was scared away from his Epistles by that great phrase in the first chapter of Romans—"the righteousness of God." He understood it then only in the cold and legal sense of justice, as a word of terror, and he declares that the word "righteousness" literally gave him a "turn of seasickness" whenever he came upon it.

The experience which opened all the windows of Luther's soul and made him both hero and reformer was his sudden discovery that God is loving and forgiving, like Christ, that instead of endeavoring to do enough works to merit salvation and satisfy the justice of God, a man needs only to see God in the light of Christ's revelation of him and in joyous faith accept his love and forgiveness. But how did he make this momentous discovery of God? How did he get to a mountainpeak where he caught that vision? It has been customary to answer: He got to his new watershed by reading and studying Saint Paul's Epistle to the Romans. The difficulty with that answer is that he had long been reading and studying Romans, but it only increased his *fear*. He read the Epistle with a veil over his eyes and heart. He needed to have the veil lifted and to see with different eyes and to feel with a different heart. It was this work of preparation for his deeper experience and vision which the mystics did for him.

Luther's first positive reference to John Tauler in his correspondence is in a letter to John Lang at Erfurt about the middle of October, 1516. He there calls the Strasbourg mystic "your Tauler," and it seems likely that John Lang had first led him to read Tauler. In the same letter Luther declares that Gabriel Biel, who was, as we have seen, once his favorite, is a "Pelagian," that is a humanist and believer in free will. Two months later (December 14) Luther wrote with enthusiasm to his friend Spalatin: "If you delight in reading pure, sound theology, like that of the earliest age, and in German, read the sermons of John Tauler, of which I send you the quintessence.[2] I have never read either in Latin or in our own tongue theology more wholesome or more agreeable to the gospel. Taste and see, therefore, how sweet is the Lord, as you have first tasted and seen how bitter is everything in us."

But we now know that Luther had for some time been reading Tauler and feeding his soul on him before he referred to him in his letters. He almost certainly had owned Tauler's sermons for a year or more before his letter to Lang. The Augsburg Edition of Tauler's sermons was issued in 1508 and Luther came into possession of a copy, probably early in 1515. He read it with glowing enthusiasm and it opened a new world to his soul. The first certain mention of him is in the *Commentary to the Romans,* which was finished in the summer of 1516. Tauler, he says, explains in the German language better than others do how God works secretly in man's heart and without his knowledge. He adds: "We do not know how to pray

---

[2] This "quintessence" is the little book of *German Theology,* which at that time Luther probably thought was written by Tauler.

as we ought. Therefore, God's strength must come to the assistance of our misery. We must acknowledge our despair and utter nakedness." He is now very much disillusioned about man's native capacities and he is leaving his easy humanism all behind. He has learned from Tauler and the "German Theology" that the human soul is deeper and more mysterious than he supposed.

Both of these fourteenth century writers put a powerful emphasis on the importance of "self-dying"—of crucifying all that pertains to the "creature." "Nothing burneth in hell," says the German Theology, "but self-will, and therefore it hath been said, put off thine own will and there will be no hell." The writer says again: "If there were no self-will, there would be no devil and no hell; and by self-will we mean willing otherwise than as the one and Eternal Will of God willeth." These mystics both call with evangelical passion and fervor for a new life to replace the old self, for a spiritual rebirth into a new creation. They offer no easy, rosy way out of the old life into the new. It is the way of Golgotha and the cross. Cost what it may of anguish and agony, the old self must die and go into the grave and rise again into newness of life—reborn and refashioned. But none of all this is *man's* work. Just here enters the unfathomable divine mystery of God's mighty love for us. He works within beyond anything we can say or think. It is a secret, hidden work of grace in the deeps of the soul and man's part is a quiet receptivity and willingness not to oppose or frustrate the inward urges of the Spirit. Another thing that Luther learned from these Friends of God was the strange truth which all great mystics know, that there come to all deep, seeking souls times of darkness and despair, when God seems to have withdrawn and to have left the soul desolate and alone crying, "My God, why hast thou forsaken me?"

These great forerunners of Luther had drained this cup of agony to the bottom. They had known what it meant to have all the fires which kindle and warm the soul go out and leave them with only cold ashes on their inner hearth. They had searched down the labyrinthine ways of their minds for some trace of the dear Presence once theirs, without finding any evidence that God was there, or that he cared about their desolation. Then in their misery and defeat they found once more in the deeps within them, that God was still there, had always been there; that his love had never let go, always suffered long and was kind, and was only completing in them the death of self and bringing about a state of utter dependence on him. They bore witness out of their own experience that love, the greatest love, is not always a soft and gentle thing. Love is bent on leading the loved one on toward perfection, and that means that there must be discipline and training; there must be the hardness and endurance that make strength and quality. They insist, therefore, that God is not harsh and angry when he seems severe. It is only the deeper and truer aspect of love revealing itself to us.

Just this lesson Luther has learned, and learned, I believe, from his new guides, the Friends of God, when he is working on his *Commentary to the Romans*. There is slight reference by name to these mystics, but their influence and their phrases are much in evidence. Luther interprets the phrase, "our tribulation worketh patience," to mean *an inward mystical tribulation.* Absolute poverty and destitution of spirit, self-annihilation and crucifixion of the will are essential steps in the path toward life in God and with God.

The surest response of Luther's mind to the appeal of German mysticism is to be found on the margins of his copy of Tauler's sermons. The volume was discovered in Zwickau in 1889 and the marginal notes were edited by Buchwald in Vol. IX of the Weimar Edition of Luther's works. Luther now holds that mystical experience is true wisdom. The highest type of religious truth is experimental truth, not doctrinal truth. He strongly stresses the necessity for human passivity and individual nothingness before God who works the miracle of the new creation in the soul that He finds ready for the divine operation. *God does everything in us.* Man is nothing; God is all. There is a strong slant toward passivity and quietism and with this tendency an immense exaltation of the immediate work of God in the soul.

Luther as usual is intense and excessive, but at the same time he reveals plainly enough that a new epoch has come in his life. His main interest is not something forensic or logical, but a genuine discovery of God. He is thoroughly disillusioned about the value of "works," of doing pious things, of trying to earn salvation, and he is now eager to let God have his unhindered way. Christ became to him now more real and intimate, more warm and tender. Religion from now on was a more heartfelt and inward matter—experience and not debates. He became more conscious now that he was to have a definite mission in God's hands and that a divinity was shaping his ends. The sacrificial note became more pronounced. The cross had broken on his sight with new meaning. There is new depth in him. He did not go all the way into the full-fledged experience of the great mystics, but he went far enough to see that the way to God is not in the sky, but in man's soul. He had no sudden invasions of the Spirit, like Pentecost, no burst of light like that which Saint Paul saw at Damascus, no voice from heaven spoke to him like the one Saint Augustine heard in the garden at Milan. But by some quiet inward process he became absolutely convinced that "God was for him" and that his salvation was assured.

He felt, to use his own vivid phrase, that he had "come under the wings of the hen." The one great experience closely akin to a mystic vision, to which Luther himself refers, is the experience which swept over him while he was working on his *Commentary to the Romans* in the Black Cloister at Wittenberg. This is the epoch-making experience which carried Luther over the watershed and made him a dynamic reformer. We used to date it in 1510; we must now date it in 1516. He had been busy for some days with that central phrase of the Epistle, "the righteousness of God." "I stood," he says, "and knocked if haply there might be someone to open unto me, but there was no one to open." He still thought of "the righteousness of God" as *justitia dei*. He supposed that it meant the *justice* of God which judges men by their deeds. The flash that came to him and changed all the values of life was the sudden insight that the righteousness of God is something *in us*—a new condition of life operating in a man. The new condition consists of the discovery of the secret of living by *faith*. When by an act of trust and confidence one looks to God for his help and believes that God is full of mercy like Christ, the miracle happens—the new life begins. Luther saw all this break forth with new light and fresh revelation when in a flash the words of Habakkuk, "the just man shall live by his faith," broke in on his soul. The man who starts living by faith is at once thereby brought into possession of the righteousness of God. His faith is the victory. The transaction is not made on the ledger-books in heaven—it is made in the soul of man. It is the discovery that man has in his own hand a key that opens a door into the storehouse of infinite love and grace which he may use whenever he will. The transformation is not in God, the transformation is in man. "When I discovered this," Luther says in his Table Talk, "I was filled with a joy passing all others." "I felt," he says elsewhere, "as though the gate of Paradise had opened wide to me." It seemed like a direct revelation of the Holy Spirit to his soul, and it set him on his sun-road, with the light on his face. It made religion for him *personal religion,* born in the deeps of the soul. That is the great experience which unhistorical tradition assigns to the holy staircase in Rome in 1510.

There is no way of proving beyond controversy that he got his insight from the mystics. He was by no means shut up to a single source of light. Father Denifle, whose range of learning is always an amazement to a student of religious history, names two hundred mediæval theologians who had interpreted the famous words, "the just shall live by his faith," pretty much as Luther did after his insight came to him. He might no doubt have caught the idea from the French Humanist Lefevre d'Etaples, whose edition of Paul's Epistles Luther used. It must be noted, however, that in spite of all his reading of theology Luther's eyes were closed to this truth and they were closed because he had grown up and had lived all his earlier life in a psychological climate which hindered him from seeing it. Whatever the star-thinkers of the church had said in their high moments, the daily practice of the church had played up schemes of debit and credit. Luther was intrenched in habits of thought which made God a hard being to deal with. His main trouble was that he was *afraid of God.* In fact, even after all his flashes of light and gleams of heavenly radiance, his fundamental thought of God was recurrently pagan and pessimistic. The best one can say of Luther is that he found now and then, here and there, a window through the black dome of his sky, but he never learned to live altogether and all the time under new heavens.

It seems pretty clear from his own comments and references that his beloved German mystics did most to pull him out of his despair into his joyous discovery. They may quite well not have been the only influence which brought his transformation, but, in the light of our present historical knowledge, they may safely be taken as the major influence. It was they who awakened him and brought new depth to his experience, a more intense glow of conviction, a greater certainty of the love of God, the reality of God's recreating work within, the necessity of personal self-surrender and crucifixion, and an eager passion to find Christ Himself as the bridegroom of the soul. The message of these passionate lovers of God bit into his life more deeply than anything else ever did, and under their touch he became the man he was—one whose supreme interest was inner religion and who cared more seriously about his relation to God than he cared for any other thing in the universe.

With the enthusiasm of a convert, Luther recommends his new-found German mystics to his friends and to his students. In the spring of 1517 he sent his copy of *German Theology* to his friend Spalatin. In his letter accompanying the copy, Luther calls the book "The Little Adam," from a phrase found in the original title of it. He goes on to say: "It is unlike anything that has ever come into my hands (I lie not) and most theological. I send it but I shall be sorry I have done so if you read it carelessly. It is beyond most learned Erasmus, and beyond Jerome, who is so much praised by him! I do not know whether they could compose such a book, *but I know they have not done so.*" In the same letter he sounds the praises of Tauler: "I beg you trust yourself to me this once, and with all your power lay hold on the book of Tauler's sermons, of which I spoke to you before. . . . From this book you will see how the learning of our age is iron or, rather, earthen, be it Greek, Latin, or Hebrew, compared to the learning of this piety." In June, 1518, Luther issued his second edition of the *German Theology*. When he brought out the earlier incomplete edition, he believed it to have been written by Tauler. He is convinced now that the authorship is unknown, the writer being called "the Frankfort Anonymous." Luther's Preface is marked by exuberant enthusiasm and praise. He declares that he has learned from it "more of what God and Christ and man are" than from any other book except the Bible and Saint Augustine. He feels that he has discovered here in the unknown prophet of Frankfort a true forerunner of his own spiritual faith.

We must turn next to ask whether Luther himself was, in any proper sense of the word, a mystic. There were, I am convinced, moments in his life, especially in those great creative years from 1515 to 1525, when he had experiences which are of the type usually called mystical. He wrote in 1521: "No one can understand God, or God's Word, unless he has it immediately revealed by the Holy

Ghost, but nobody can receive anything from the Holy Ghost unless he *experiences* it. In experience the Holy Ghost teaches as in his own school, outside of which nothing can be learned." That passage has the hall-mark of the mystic and would fit into the pages of any sermon by Tauler or Eckhart. So too would these words, on the mystical union through faith, fit into the writings of any great mystic: "Faith has the incomparable grace of uniting the soul to Christ as bride to husband, so that the soul possesses whatever Christ himself possesses."

There are many other passages of like import in Luther's early Tracts, and there are good evidences that he was often made joyous and radiant by the overmastering consciousness of God's invading love. But it must, nevertheless, be admitted that, while he was guided far on his perilous journey by the hands of the mystics who preceded him, and while he had some rare mystic moments and inner insights, he was not temperamentally or constitutionally a mystic. Then as soon as the Spiritual Reformers, the Anabaptists, and the uprising Peasants revealed to him the explosive character of his original faith-idea and the antinomian perils with which the uncharted inward way was fraught, Luther swung over strongly toward the safer method of an ancient *authority*. But in spite of this, to the end of his life, he owed a great debt to "the Friends of God" who *found* him in his youth and helped him to discover his way through the jungle, and he never quite lost his capacity to rise to experiences which made him "joyous and intrepid," and in the strength of which he could "die a thousand deaths."

One of the most vital interpreters of Luther's faith was Wilhelm Herrmann, of Marburg, Germany, with whom I studied in 1911. He was an illuminating teacher and all his writings reveal the pure and noble quality of his spirit. But he was always a militant opponent of "mysticism." I had at least one memorable debate with him on this issue, he speaking in German and I in English. His whole contention is presented with depth and vigor in his very valuable book, *The Communion of the Christian With God*.

Here we can discover at once where the trouble lies. "Mysticism" for Herrmann was a straight and narrow path by which the soul, unaided by any helps of Scripture, history, church literature, saintly guides, or external nature, rose as by a miracle to a lonely beatific vision of God—infinite, absolute, perfect Being, but at the same time "pure," that is, without concrete character, abstract, and empty. "Mysticism," as he defined it, was "devoid of the positive content of any soul-dominating idea, giving rise to thoughts that elevate the spiritual life." It is the experience of an almighty *Blank*. It is a vague and surging impression of contact with a glorified Nothing-in-Particular, but spelled with capitals and thought of as standing for the All.

Herrmann proceeds to show that one who dedicates his life to this quest abandons everything else, and so "steps outside the pale of truly Christian piety." Quoting Harnack, who agrees with this thin and truncated view of mysticism, he says: "These [mystics] always lacked their full momentum *so long as they took any notice of anything whatever that was outside of God and the soul*" (italics mine). Herrmann thereupon proceeds to set forth a type of religion which brings the soul into "actual communion with God" of such a sort that the person who has the experience is constrained to say, "This is God." In this quest for God, which Herrmann approves as the highest quest, and in which he himself was a devoted pilgrim, the seeker does not cut himself loose from history through which God has revealed himself, nor from spiritual literature, nor, above all, from "the human Jesus, in whom we meet with a fact whose content is incomparably richer than that of any feelings which arise within ourselves."

We shall, according to Herrmann, regard as "revelation" everything "which brings us into actual communion with God." This experience, he grants, will "culminate in the ineffable," but the experience will at the same time have all the spiritual content of the stages of the revelation that has brought us to it. It will not be a "blank"; it will be rich with the concrete truth of history, literature, life, and especially with the "deepened moral consciousness that has been produced by the revelation of God in Jesus Christ."

Herrmann proceeds in a masterly manner to set forth the way in which the personal life of Christ, grasped as a reality, becomes *a saving fact,* inwardly transforms the soul, raises the believer out of darkness into light, out of weakness into strength, out of fear into joy, and finally into living union and communion with God. Herrmann finds in this way of faith the key to Luther's experience and to Luther's reforming idea—"Trust in Christ means to Luther *the actual experience of redemption.*"

I am in hearty accord with Herrmann's deep and penetrating study of the experience of communion with God. I agree with him that a "mysticism" which rejects concrete helps, turns away from historical revelation, and which focuses upon a blank is of doubtful worth. But I do not see why mysticism should be limited and confined to this blank and sterile procedure. Most of what Herrmann means by the experience of communion is what I mean by mysticism. He insists that without this deeper inward experience of communion with God "there can be no religion at all," so that for *him* "religion" means what mysticism means for *me.*

It is a fact, nevertheless, that religion is marked with immense variations, and we need a word to cover the intense, the first-hand, the inward and immediate religious experiences, and the word mystical quite properly applies to those varieties of religion.

A large part of religion in the course of history has been *forensic,* and this is peculiarly true of Luther's religion and that of the other reformers. By forensic religion I mean that type of religion that attributes an efficacious value to sacred words, phrases, doctrines, creeds, and performances. Here we have to do, not with the warm and intimate experience of something actually occurring within, but with a *belief* that the use of sacred words, the performance of certain acts, the acceptance of mental attitudes and positions are bound to work desirable results upon the destiny of the soul. These results are not *experienced,* but they are *believed in* and *taken as real.* This is very close to what we often call "authoritative religion." Many a person—and Luther is a striking example—have both of these two types of religion, the mystical and the forensic, strongly in evidence in their lives. There are too, of course, many other aspects of religion which have a specific name and a recognized standing. The metaphysical approach to religion, and by no means of least importance, the ethical approach would both need to be sounded out if this were the place for it.

I am contending here that the word "mystical" stands for a very important aspect of historic religion—just that aspect which has to do with direct and first-hand experience of God; that it includes and covers what Herrmann calls "the experience of actual communion with God," and equally well those great experiences of Luther's by which through an inward act of faith he found himself flooded with joy, united with God, and raised to a new level of energy and power. A large part of Luther's contribution is in the sphere of what I have called forensic religion, but there are signal times and places when a living contact is made, when his whole inner being burns, like Moses' bush, with divine fire, when God becomes as real to him as the Wartburg, and when he feels that he can stand the universe, both visible and invisible. Such experiences, whether they are found in John Tauler, or the Frankfort Anonymous, or in Martin Luther—and they sometimes are found in him—are rightly designated mystical experiences.

V

MYSTICISM IN ROBERT BROWNING

WHEN Sir Ernest Shackleton was starting out on his last journey of exploration in the antarctic, he made the statement that the poetry of Robert Browning had been the greatest inspiration of his life. The special points which Shackleton singled out for emphasis were Browning's message of faith in the rational significance of things, his bugle note of optimism, and his constant call to courage and to action. There are many of us that have never gone out to discover the earth's poles or even to climb Himalayas who can also say that Browning's poetry has been an immense stimulus and inspiration to our lives. It is difficult for some of us quite to conceive what life would have been without his clarion call.

When we ask why he, more than other optimists, raises our responsive faith and creates within us an abounding courage for life and action, the answer almost certainly is that he more than most poets had a basic conception of the universe which made an optimistic outlook sound and rational—a foundation belief on which a man could dare to live. It is true, no doubt, that he possessed an optimistic temperament to begin with. And that counts for much. When he turned to his world and searched it for informing facts, he found nothing in the universe absolutely bad and hopeless.

"Of absolute and irretrievable
  And all-subduing black—black's soul of black,
  Beyond white's power to disintensify—
  Of that I saw no sample: such may wreck
  My life and ruin my philosophy."
                    ("A Bean Stripe.")

But his optimism ran down far below his observations and rested upon his indubitable conviction that God is not only real but everywhere living and operative, and not only all-powerful but perfect in love as well.

"God! Thou art love! I build my faith on that."
                    ("Paracelsus.")
"I say the acknowledgment of God in Christ
  Accepted by thy reason, solves for thee
  All questions in the earth and out of it."
                    ("A Death in the Desert.")

This fundamental acknowledgment he himself had made; he had made it as an act of his reason, and that grounded faith of his made him able to stand all kinds of cosmic weather—even the waterspouts and euroclydons. So confident was he of the stabilizing and curative forces in the world that he rather enjoyed the dangers and risks that beset the voyager here. He gloried in the perilous and rejoiced in the hazardous, dramatic ventures of life.

"Then, welcome each rebuff
  That turns earth's smoothness rough,
  Each sting that bids nor sit nor stand but go!"

    . . . .

Machinery just meant
To give thy soul its bent,
Try thee and turn thee forth, sufficiently impressed."
             ("Rabbi Ben Ezra.")

As I have said, this deep-lying faith of his rested upon a seasoned philosophy which he held. There was a strong Kantian strand in him as there was too, in Tennyson, and prophet as he was, he had leaped at once to the immense significance of the principle of evolution, a potency working all things up to better. But, as I hope to show in this paper, Browning also had at the nether basis of his faith a very important strand of first-hand, mystical experience. He seems to be speaking in the first person when he says,

> "Where one heard noise,
> And one saw flame,
> I only knew He named my name."
> ("Christmas Eve.")

Browning was not a mystic in the same sense that his great contemporary, Tennyson, was. Tennyson's account of his own unusual psychical experience is an interesting one. He wrote: "A kind of waking trance—this for lack of a better word—I have frequently had quite up from my boyhood when I have been alone. This has come upon me through repeating my own name to myself silently, till all at once, as it were out of the intensity of the consciousness of individuality, individuality itself seemed to dissolve and fade away into boundless being, and this not a confused state, but the clearest, the surest of the surest, utterly beyond words—where death was an almost laughable impossibility—the loss of personality (if so it were) seeming no extinction, but the only true life." There are marks of this and other psychical experiences to be found in many of Tennyson's poems. "It is," he once said to John Tyndall, "no nebulous ecstasy, but a state of transcendent wonder, associated with absolute clearness of mind."

So far as I have been able to discover, Browning showed no tendency to trance or ecstasy. He was normal in his mental processes and not "psychically," that is, psychopathically, disposed. If he had such experiences, he kept them to himself, locked in his own heart. He consumed his own smoke. He did not approve of a poet's unlocking his heart and throwing it wide open for the public to see in and scrutinize all its processes.

"A peep through the window, if folks prefer;
But please you, no foot over threshold of mine."

He did not like the purveyors of psychic mysteries, and he was rationally suspicious of mediums and those who "guess what's going on outside the veil." "Men spin clouds of fuzz where matters end" ("Bishop Blougram's Apology").

Here is his diagnosis of the value of the judgment of a spectator at a seance and his ability to distinguish between trick and the real appearance in the case of a certain child who died:

"And whose last breath you thought your lips had felt:

. . . .

The little voice set lisping once again,
The tiny hand made feel for yours once more,
The poor lost image brought back, plain as dreams,
Which image, if a word had chanced recall,
The customary cloud would cross your eyes,
Your heart return the old tick, pay its pang!
A right mood for investigation, this!
One's at one's ease with Saul and Jonathan,
Pompey and Cæsar: but one's own lost child. . .
I wonder, when you heard the first clod drop
From the spadeful at the grave-side, felt you free
To investigate who twitched your funeral scarf
Or brushed your flounces? Then, it came of course,
You should be stunned and stupid; then (how else?)
Your breath stopped with your blood, your brain struck work.

But now, such causes fail of such effects,
All's changed—the little voice begins afresh,
Yet you, calm, consequent, can test and try,
And touch the truth."
  ("Mr. Sludge, 'The Medium.'")

But while he was healthily normal, rationally minded, critical of unusual phenomena, he yet was in the truest and best sense of the word a mystic—a person who had first-hand experiences of God and could say with his John in the desert, "I saw."

I shall endeavor to show from his own words how deep and vital this first-hand experience of God was in Browning's case, and I shall also show how he performed another service of great importance in his flashes about the nature of the soul. This latter service is one which we peculiarly need at the present moment, when there is perhaps more skepticism over the existence of the soul than there is over the existence of God. Mrs. Browning wrote of Lucretius,

"Who dropped his plummet down the broad
  Deep universe and said, 'No God,'
Finding no bottom."

Her husband was always dropping his plummet down the abysmal deeps of the human soul and concluding that there must be a God, just because the soul proved to be bottomless. I shall deal first with his testimony of acquaintance with God.

You have a man talking out of real experience in words like these:

". . . . . . 'I,
Who want, am made for, and must have a God
Ere I can be aught, do aught—no mere name
Want, but the true thing with what proves its
     truth,
To-wit, a relation from that thing to me,
Touching from head to foot—which touch I feel,
And with it take the rest, this life of ours!'"
     ("Bishop Blougram's Apology.")

Or those other words of his:

That one Face, far from vanish, rather grows,
Or decomposes but to recompose,
Becomes my universe that feels and knows!
     (Epilogue.)

His was a mysticism of the best affirmation type, which, after centuries of intellectual and spiritual travail, has found a better way than the *via negativa*, whose terminus was "the Dark," or "the nameless Nothing," or "the naked Godhead where there is never form or idea"—"the Wilderness where no one is at home," as the great negation mystics call the goal of all our search. This new mysticism builds solidly upon the normal experiences of man's soul. It insists upon the truth that the Beyond which we are forever seeking is within ourselves. In fact, we are seeking just because in some sense we have already found God. We so tiny and he so great are inherently kin and belong to one common spiritual universe. He is the foundation of all that is real and spiritual. As Browning puts it:

"Take all in a word: the truth in God's breast
  Lies trace for trace upon ours impressed:
  Though he is so bright and we so dim,
  We are made in his image to witness him."
                    ("Christmas Eve.")

"The child feels God a moment, (then) ichors o'er the place," he says. The main trouble with us elders, it would seem, is that the ichor has grown to be a hardened scar over what might be called the sensitive spots of the soul.

Not only is God behind the soul for him, the environment of it, as the water is for the swimming fish, but he is in a similar way the foundational basis and life of everything else. Take this passage from "Sludge" as a sample:

"We find great things are made of little things,
   And little things go lessening till at last
   Comes God behind them. Talk of mountains now?
   We talk of mold that heaps the mountains, mites
   That throng the mold, and God that makes the mites.
   The Name comes close behind a stomach-cyst,
   The simplest of creations, just a sac
   That's mouth, heart, legs and belly at once, yet lives
   And feels, and could do neither, we conclude,
   If simplified still further one degree:
   The small becomes the dreadful and immense!"
      ("Mr. Sludge, 'The Medium.'")

Browning has often been supposed to be a rationalist and philosopher among poets. That is not a sound position. A rationalist is not a poet—he is a rationalist. Browning was a full natured, all-around man. He did not cut asunder his emotional life from his intellectual. He loved with his whole mind as well as with his heart and strength. He stood for the integral life. A whole man can be a poet, but not a man who proposes to use only that little fragment of himself which he calls his "rationalizing faculty." He once wrote:

". . . to know *is* something, and to prove
  How all this beauty might be enjoyed, is more:
  But, knowing naught, to enjoy is something too."
                                    ("Cleon.")

And this living word from *Luria* is drawn from his own deep experience:

"God glows above,
With scarce any intervention presses close,
And palpitatingly His soul o'er ours!
We feel him, nor by painful reason know."

But, as I have pointed out, when Browning says "feel him," and exalts that method of approach in place of slow and painful rationalization, he is not setting emotions over against reason, as a better source of knowledge. He is insisting upon the great fact that the spirit of man, in its unified and total being, can partake of God and does discover that His Spirit presses palpitatingly over and around ours.

"Rejoice, we are allied
To that which doth provide.

. . . .

Nearer we hold of God
Who gives, than of his tribes that take."
("Rabbi Ben Ezra.")

That is precisely what the sane affirmative mystic means by mysticism. God and man are allied, are kin. Man is not sundered, and cannot be sundered from God any more than a division of space can be sundered from space as a whole. As soon as we get cured, if we ever do, of the habit of thinking of God in terms of the ancient Ptolemaic astronomy, as though he lived off somewhere above the crystalline dome of the sky, while we live far beneath him on this dull, sober earth, we shall find it easier to be mystics. We shall realize, as so many do not now, that there is only one place where God can be found in his full meaning and that is where beauty is found, and consciousness is found, and goodness is found, and love is found, and sacrifice is found, and personality is found. We shall expect of star-wheels and planets only what can be expressed in terms of masses and energies and velocities.

We shall find in the slowly ascending spiral of life and in the long dramatic processes of history a revelation of God, to be sure, but these revelations, external to us, will always lack the warm, intimate, and personal factor. Up to that point God will always seem somewhat foreign to us. It is when we find him palpitatingly close about our own souls that we can say, "I have seen," and "The God of the universe is my God." We rise to a first-hand religion when we can say, as he says, in "Christmas Eve,"

> "His All in All appears serene
> With the thinnest human veil between,
> Letting the mystic lamps, the seven,
> The many motions of His Spirit,
> Pass, as they list, to earth from heaven."

Then, to use his vigorous figure in the same poem, we feel "our soul's depth boil in earnest."

It is this immense transition from the God of the cosmos to the God of intimate personal experience that is expressed in another fine passage of "Christmas Eve," which is one of the most personal of all his poems. He says:

"In youth I looked to these very skies,
And probing their immensities,
I found God there, his visible power;
Yet felt in my heart, amid all its sense
Of the power, an equal evidence
That his love, there too, was the nobler dower.
For the loving worm within its clod,
Were diviner than a loveless God
Amid his worlds, I will dare to say."

It is not necessary here to reiterate what every lover—in fact, almost every reader—of Browning knows, that love as the essential character of God is a central theme of Browning's and is emphasized in a very large number of his poems. It is a recurrent note from the beginning to the end of his literary period. He found evidence of it in strange and unusual types, and he put his message about it in the mouth of odd and bizarre witnesses, but in the last analysis his faith in the Love of God rests upon his own experience of it. It is the testimony of his own heart.

"I have faith such end shall be:
From the first, Power was—I knew.
Life has made clear to me
That strive for closer view,
Love were as plain to see." ("Reverie.")

That is not something which surged into his consciousness as a sudden invasion. It did not come up like a subterranean upheaval or uprush from his subliminal self. He did not return from an ecstasy and bring this "find," as the diver brings his pearl from his plunge—

"A beggar, he prepares to plunge;
A prince, he rises with his pearl."
("Paracelsus.")

Not that way. "Truth may be flashed out by one blow," no doubt, but it is more often won by the slow gestation and maturing of normal experience. Spiritual truth, certainty of God, the immense significance of Christ, the living contacts of the Holy Spirit, are attained as appreciation of beauty is attained, as artistic taste is gained, as tact is acquired, as moral insight is won, by the slow accumulation of experience which saves its gains and out of them builds a character that knows by second nature. Here is the way Caponsacchi puts it:

"To have to do with nothing but the true,
 The good, the eternal—and these, not alone
 In the main current of the general life,

But small experiences of every day,
Concerns of the particular hearth and home:
To learn not only by a comet's rush
But a rose's birth—not by the grandeur, God—
But the comfort, Christ."
>   ("The Ring and the Book.")

It is thus that this sensitive inner spirit is formed. The only reason for calling this method of attaining truth mystical is that we are dealing here with "knowledge of acquaintance" and not with "knowledge about," with first-hand experience and not with second-hand, with what is inwardly apprehended and not with what is externally communicated. And Browning's poetry is pretty well crammed with matter of first-hand experience because inwardly apprehended. In any case this inwardly formed and spiritually tested conviction of his came to be absolutely sure.

> "The flesh I wear,
> The earth I tread, are not more clear to me
> Than by belief. If I stoop
> Into a dark, tremendous sea of cloud,
> It is but for a time; I press God's lamp
> Close to my breast; its splendor, soon or late,
> Will pierce the gloom."
>   ("Paracelsus.")

He had a working theory that the main source of truth is, after all, within the soul. The classical passage which interprets this mystical source of truth is, of course, the famous one in "Paracelsus," and it is a capital example of the interpretation of the point of view which it has been my purpose to develop above:

"Truth is within ourselves; it takes no rise
  From outward things, whate'er you may believe.
  There is an inmost center in us all,
  Where truth abides in fullness; and around,
  Wall upon wall, the gross flesh hems it in,
  This perfect, clear perception—which is truth;
  A baffling and perverting carnal mesh
  Binds it and makes all error: and, *to Know*
  Rather consists in opening out a way
  Whence the imprisoned splendor may escape,
  Than in effecting entry for a light
  Supposed to be without. Watch narrowly
  The demonstration of a truth, its birth,
  And you trace back the effluence to its spring
  And source within us; where broods radiance vast,
To be elicited, ray by ray."

The same idea comes out forcibly in Saint John's words in the poem, "A Death in the Desert."

"Can they share
—They, who have flesh, a veil of youth and strength
About each spirit, that needs must bide its time,
Living and learning still as years assist,
Which wear the thickness thin, and let man see—
With me who hardly am withheld at all,
But shudderingly, scarce a shred between,
Lie bare to the universal prick of light?
Is it for nothing we grow old and weak,
We whom God loves?"

There is another passage to the same effect in the soliloquy of the venerable Pope—now in his

"gray ultimate decrepitude—
Yet sensible of fires that more and more
Visit a soul, in passage to the sky,
Left nakeder than when flesh-robe was new."

His remarkable bracket in that great Christian poem already quoted, "A Death in the Desert," gives a profoundly mystical interpretation of the nature of the soul. It is an ancient view of the great mystics, but apparently Browning holds it himself, or something like it—a divine apex to the soul which connects it in unsundered fashion with God. There is first the soul which represents the life of the body; then there is the soul, which

"Feeleth, thinketh, willeth—is what *knows*.
 Which, duly tending upward in its turn,
 Grows into, and again is grown into
 By the last soul, which uses both the first,
 Subsisting whether they assist or no,
 And, constituting man's self, is what Is—
 And leans upon the former, makes it play,
 As that played off the first: and, tending up,
 Holds, is upheld by, God, and ends the man
 Upward in that dread point of intercourse,
 Nor needs a place, for it returns to him."

It was a conception of man's soul like that which gave the mystics of the fourteenth century the ground of their spiritual faith. Aristotle supplied them with the basis for their theory of the soul, but this highest self of Browning, which ends the man upward "in that dread point of intercourse," is bolder than Aristotle dared to be, and is of a piece with Eckhart's famous doctrine of the *Fünklein*, or "flash," at the apex of man's inner self.

It is just because our lives are so closely joined with the life of God that we in our earthly sphere, with our varied experiences, can be organs of God to others. As Pompilia says:

> "Through such souls alone
> God stooping shows sufficient of his light
> For us i' the dark to rise by."

The Pope, in "The Ring and the Book," gives a very interesting review of the new movement in religion, which is going on around him in his old age, led by the mystic Molinists, with whom he himself deeply sympathizes. He sees the danger of trusting the inward promptings of the spirit in place of the safe assurance of ancient creeds and age-long customs, but he wonders whether this risky and hazardous way of life which throws decision on the individual soul and makes a man "stand out again, pale, resolute, prepared to die," will not mean really fresh life and power in place of the torpor that has come with safety and dull routine. He welcomes the step which means "faith in the thing itself" in place of "faith in the report" of the reality, that is, first-hand instead of second-hand faith. He shows how these mystics of his time peril their bodies and their souls too in obedience to truths revealed within themselves—"unrecognized yet, but perceptible," and resolve by this light in their souls to

"Correct the portrait by the living Face,
  Man's God by God's God in the mind of man."

Then it is that Browning introduces that fine figure of the person who knows "the right place by the foot's feel." Many a time as a boy I have found my way home at night, in the country, when it was too dark to see a single sign or pointer, by letting my feet find the road beneath. That, the old Pope says, is to be the new way. Already, he says, there are "experimentalists in the new order" who carry their guide within themselves and who will be for the new age what Saint Augustine was for the old. He sees risks and dangers in this looser, more fluid type of religion, but, on the whole, he votes for it, and he is sure that the nobler spirits will obey God, find the right path, and be victorious in the hard choices of life. Pompilia is his sample flower of the new order:

"Everywhere
I see in the world the intellect of man,
That sword, the energy his subtle spear,
The knowledge that defends him like a shield—
Everywhere; but they make not up, I think,

> The marvel of a soul like thine, earth's flower
> She holds up to the softened gaze of God."

One who did right because her pure soul *saw and knew*.

There is, then, the possibility of forming within the soul a subtle, swift, sure sense of spiritual direction as infallible as that of the homing bird or the migrating wild goose, and with it a consciousness of response to that wider environing Spirit which surrounds the soul as the ocean does the island. "So," says the ripened old Pope,

> "So, never I miss footing in the maze,
>   No—I have light, nor fear the dark at all."

This is quite obviously not the mysticism of the great negatives or of the great ecstatics, nor does it present the well-defined ladders and scales of the systematic mystics, like Saint John of the Cross. It is that better, modern, normal type that builds upon the kinship between man and God, and finds all life shot through with divine possibilities and linked up in its deepest strata with the foundational sources of life in God.

> "This is the glory—that in all conceived,
>   Or felt or known, I recognize a *mind*

Not mine but like mine—for the double joy—
Making all things for me and me, for Him."
("Prince Hohenstiel-Schwangau.")

Sometimes a "bar is broken between," the bar that keeps us outside and isolated, and for blessed moments—"moments sure though seldom," he says, we see and hear and feel and find our contact, "In spite of the mortal screen" ("By the Fireside"). There are a few who, by stricter training and completer obedience, have brought themselves into parallelism with celestial currents, and *they* have the experimental touch. "God has a few of us whom He whispers in the ear" (Abt Vogler). Practice of the spiritual life perfects this strange stringed instrument of ours and makes it a better and ever better organ of the Spirit of God. Even the stubborn body, the somewhat recalcitrant "brother ass" that carries the soul, can be molded into a finer, fitter nature, until we are able to cry with joy and enthusiasm:

"All good things
Are ours, nor soul helps flesh more, now, than flesh helps soul."
("Rabbi Ben Ezra.")

The organizing process goes forward day by day until even old-time liabilities become positive spiritual assets and count on the right side of the ledger.

"All instincts immature,
All purposes unsure,

. . . .

Thoughts hardly to be packed
Into a narrow act,
Fancies that broke through language and escaped;
All I could never be,
All men ignored in me,
This, I was worth to God, whose wheel the pitcher shaped."

This quickening of life, this subtle sensitizing of the soul and harmonizing of the body into an attuned organ of the divine life is what Browning often dealt with. You get this kind of harmonized person in the great passage I now quote:

"The one royal race
That ever was, or will be, in this world!
They give no gift that bounds itself and ends
I' the giving and the taking: theirs so breeds
I' the heart and soul o' the taker, so transmutes
The man who only was a man before,
That he grows godlike in his turn, can give—

He also; share the poets' privilege,
Bring forth new good, new beauty, from the old."
("Balaustion's Adventure.")

This calm, ordered, normal consciousness of God and of fellowship with him is a well-known characteristic of the poetry of this robust and stimulating optimist of the Victorian era. There are times, however, when the intensity heightens and the spiritual passion glows with white heat, and the reader feels that the poet is giving a glimpse of intimate experiences which go far toward the rapturous and ecstatic state. At least, if he has not had these experiences himself, he knows how to express them vividly in others.

"Novel splendors burst forth, grew familiar and dwelt with mine.

. . . .

Nay more; for there wanted not who walked in the glare and glow,
Presences plain in the place.

. . . .

What never had been, was now; what was, as it shall be anon;
And what is—shall I say matched both? for I was made perfect too."
("Abt Vogler.")

Or this:

> "With life forever old yet new,
> Changed not in kind but in degree,
> The instant made eternity."
> ("The Last Ride Together.")

The rapture which came with David's sublime discovery, in "Saul":

> "The stars of night beat with emotion and tingled and shot
> Out in fire the strong pain of pent knowledge; but I fainted not,
> For the Hand still impelled me at once and supported, suppressed
> All the tumult, and quenched it with quiet, and holy behest,
> Till the rapture was shut in itself, and the earth sank to rest."

One more deeply emotional passage, describing human life caught up and enveloped in the wider, diviner Life to which we belong:

> "The whole Face turned upon me full,
> And I spread myself beneath it,
> As when the bleacher spreads, to seethe it
> In the cleansing sun, his wool—
> Steeps in the flood of moontide whiteness
> Some defiled, discolored web—
> So lay I, saturate with brightness."
> ("Christmas Eve.")

VI

THE MYSTICAL ELEMENT IN WALT WHITMAN

I AM a late arrival in the ever-growing group of those who appreciate Walt Whitman. I bore no burdens and suffered no reproaches during the heat of the day. It is only at the eleventh hour that I have heeded the call to work in his vineyard. I remained for years cold to his type of poetry, and puritanic, if not pharisaic, toward what I thought were his social theories and his way of life. I am joining the laborers now not in order to get the "penny" which I do not deserve, but solely because in these later and richer years of my life I have been in some true sense discovering the real man that he was and I have been learning to appreciate the depth of insight, the naked sincerity, the spirit of brotherhood, the passion for simplicity, the glowing love of country and humanity that were essential to his soul, and at the same time the extraordinary quality of poetic genius that is revealed in his creative work. He was trying all his life with all his might to save America from materialism and materialistic aims.

In the days of my pride and ignorance I should have laughed to scorn anyone who had suggested hunting for a lofty mystical strand in the author of *Leaves of Grass*. It would have seemed in that period of prejudice like searching for sunlight in dark cellars and in windowless ghettos. But that judgment would have been due to blank ignorance, not to the absence of the mystical strand, for there it was and is as plain to see as the harvest moon in October.

Dr. R. M. Bucke, of Canada, was one of the first of the Whitman lovers to dwell upon this noble element of mysticism in the poet. He visited Whitman in 1877 and was "almost amazed by the beauty and majesty of his person and the gracious air of purity that surrounded and permeated him." He seemed to Doctor Bucke to be in some sense clearly and entirely a unique being, and that brief visit, during which Whitman spoke only about a hundred words, was the turning point in the famous doctor's life.[1] Shortly

[1] *Walt Whitman Fellowship Papers*, VI, Sept., 1894.

after leaving the poet, Doctor Bucke, in his simple account of the experience, says that "a state of mental exaltation set in . . . an exaltation that lasted at least six weeks in a clearly marked degree," and it left behind a permanent element in his life, "a strong and living force, making for purity and happiness." "I may add," Doctor Bucke continues, speaking of himself in the third person, "that this person's whole life has been changed by that contact—his temper, character, entire spiritual being, outer life, conversation, etc., elevated and purified in an extraordinary degree."[2]

Emerson, America's foremost living mystic in the middle years of the nineteenth century, was the first person to recognize Whitman's genius. This was in 1855, twenty-two years before Doctor Bucke discovered him. It was Whitman's extraordinary energy, what we should now call his *élan vital,* that at once impressed the Sage of Concord—"the buffalo strength" and "terrible eyes" of the new poet. "I greet you at the beginning of a great career," Emerson wrote to Whitman in 1855, "which

---

[2] *Cosmic Consciousness*, p. 180.

yet must have had a long foreground somewhere, for such a start. I rubbed my eyes a little to see if this sunbeam were no illusion." Emerson makes no mention at this early stage of Whitman's mystical quality, though he notes it, as he would be sure to do, in later comments.

It is an urgent task, of course, to explain what is meant by the cryptic phrase, "mystical element." It may mean almost anything, divine or diabolical. Its presence in a writer would send some readers to his books with a holy enthusiasm; it would lead others to use the same books as kindling material for the grate. For some it means "emotional slush"; for others it signifies "celestial efflatus." In the minds of some it betokens psychopathic hysteria, and for others it will indicate an oracular soul in contact with God. Emerson once remarked humorously that *Leaves of Grass* was a combination of the *Bhagavad Gita* and the New York Herald. It would be possible under this rubric of "mystical element" to make even more bizarre combinations than that which Emerson suggested!

Doctor Bucke introduced into our vocabulary a new word for this much abused term, "mystical." He called this peculiar type of experience "cosmic consciousness." "Cosmic consciousness" means for him a unique and higher form of consciousness as much above ordinary self-consciousness as that is above the simple consciousness of the animal or the child. By means of this higher consciousness a person breaks through the veils and husks of the universe and comes into living experience of the inner heart of things.

> "And hears the bubbling of the springs
> That feed the world."

There occurs, to use Doctor Bucke's own language, "an intellectual enlightenment or illumination, which alone would place the individual on a new plane of existence—would make him almost a member of a new species. To this is added a state of moral exaltation, an indescribable feeling of elevation, elation and joyousness, and a quickening of the moral sense, which is fully as striking as and more important both to the individual and to the race than is the enhanced intellectual power. With these come what may be called a sense of immortality, a consciousness of eternal life, not a conviction that he *shall* have this, but the consciousness that he *has* it already."[3]

Emerson in his essays on *Nature* and on the *Oversoul* had prepared the way for "cosmic consciousness." "There is," Emerson wrote in the *Oversoul,* "no bar or wall in the soul, where man the effect ceases and where God the cause begins. The walls are taken away. We lie open on one side to the deeps of spiritual nature, to the attributes of God." When this Oversoul breathes through man's intellect, "it is genius; when it breathes through his will, it is virtue; when it flows through his affections it is love." Emerson's writings, both prose and poetry, are full of mystical thought suggested or expressed, and he everywhere assumes a universal mind operating above us and through us—"an influx of the divine mind into our mind." In fact, Emerson was the stimulating and creative influence behind both Whitman and Doctor Bucke, for Emerson introduced a *new factor* into American life and thought.

F. W. H. Myers, of England, who first

---
[3] *Cosmic Consciousness*, p. 2.

used the term "subliminal consciousness" for what Doctor Bucke called "cosmic consciousness," described mystical experience as the experience of "the coexistence and interpenetration of a real or spiritual with the material or phenomenal world: a belief driven home to many minds by experiences both more weighty and more concordant than the percipients themselves have always known—the veritable nascency, and operation of 'a last and largest sense'; a faculty for apprehending, not God indeed (for what finite faculty can apprehend the Infinite?) but at least some dim and scattered tokens and prefigurements of a true world of Life and Love."[4]

Whitman does not use the vocabulary of these interpreters of mysticism, but he reveals a tendency of thought, the subsoil of which is similar to that in Coleridge, Emerson, Carlyle, and in the transcendental mystics of the early nineteenth century. There is an underlying strand of thought in them all that has come, usually unconsciously, from Fichte, Schelling, Goethe, and the German Romanticists. The soul has a bot-

[4] *Human Personality*, vol. ii, p. 286.

tomless depth because it "lies open on one side to the infinite deeps of spiritual nature." The interesting thing about a genius is the fact that in some mysterious way he feels out and discovers what fits and feeds the appetite and aptitudes of his soul, as bees find the distant clover which holds the honey they need for their hive. Whitman very early found the nether springs which supplied him for the rest of his life, and from 1853 onward he knew, by a kind of infallible insight, that Jacob's ladder goes up to the highest height from the apex of man's soul. Take this little poem of Whitman's, first printed in 1870, as an illustration of the way in which he believes that the soul, out of its inmost self, can reach across all chasms and make its contacts with the environing Large Life.

"A noiseless, patient spider,
  I marked, where, on a little promontory, it stood, isolated;
  Marked how, to explore the vacant, vast surrounding,
  It launched forth filament, filament, filament, out of itself;
  Ever unreeling them—ever tirelessly speeding them,

And you, O my Soul, where you stand,
Surrounded, surrounded, in measureless oceans of space,
Ceaselessly musing, venturing, throwing—seeking the spheres, to connect them;
Till the bridge you will need, be formed—till the ductile anchor hold;
Till the gossamer thread you fling, catch somewhere,
O my Soul."[5]

In the "Song of the Universal" he finds the Soul to be the one stupendous reality "amid the measureless grossness and slag."

"Yet again, lo! the Soul—above all science;
For it, has History gathered like a husk around the globe;
For it, the entire star-myriads roll through the sky.
In spiral roads, by long detours,
(As a much-tacking ship upon the sea).
For it, the partial to the permanent flowing,
For it, the Real to the Ideal tends.
For it, the mystic evolution."

"O the blest eyes! the happy hearts!
That see—that know the guiding thread so fine,
Along the mighty labyrinth!"

---

[5] All quotations from Walt Whitman's works are reprinted by permission of Doubleday, Doran and Company, publishers.

Then comes this great burst of prophetic insight:

"Give me, O God, to sing that thought!
　Give me—give him or her I love, this quenchless faith
　In thy ensemble. Whatever else withheld, withhold not from us
　Belief in plan of thee enclosed in Time and Space;
　　Health, peace, salvation universal.

Is it a dream?
Nay, but the lack of it the dream,
And, failing it, life's lore and wealth a dream,
And all the world a dream."

But Whitman not only had a fundamental theory of life and of the world that favored a mystical outlook and interpretation; he had besides a psychical disposition which inclined him to mystical experiences —incursions from beyond what seemed the margins of himself. He came also early in his life under Quaker influences which had an important shaping effect on what I have called the subsoil of his inner nature. He has described in his essay on Elias Hicks how as a small boy he was taken to Quaker meeting by his father and mother, "as a special reward," "as I had been behaving well that day." He found himself in "perfect silence" which he elsewhere has called "noiseless silent ecstasy," and then Elias Hicks preached with "a pleading, tender, nearly agonizing conviction," and in "a magnetic stream of natural eloquence before which all minds and natures, all emotions, high or low, gentle or simple, yielded entirely without exception." "It was not argumentative or intellectual, but penetrating—different from anything in books." He calls the preaching of Hicks "mystical," and he means by it "the old Platonic doctrine that the ideals of character, of justice, of religious action, whenever the highest is at stake, are to be conformed to no outward doctrine of creeds, Bibles, legislative enactments, conventionalities, or even decorums, but are to follow *the inward, Deity-planted law of the emotional soul.*"

In a brief essay entitled "George Fox and Shakespeare," Whitman has vividly expressed what he owed to the Quaker tradition and to the Quaker way of life, and he has dared to put the Drayton shoemaker side by side with the great Elizabethan dramatist. They were born and bred, he says, "of similar stock in much the same surroundings and station in life." But "what," he asks, "is poor plain George Fox compared to William Shakespeare—to fancy's lord, imagination's heir?" "Yet George Fox stands for something too—a thought—the thought that wakes in silent hours—perhaps the deepest, most eternal thought latent in the human soul. This is the thought of God, merged in the thoughts of moral right and the immortality of identity. Great, great is this thought—aye, greater than all else. When the gorgeous pageant of Art, refulgent in the sunshine, color'd with roses and gold—with all the richest mere poetry, old or new (even Shakespeare's)—with all that statue, play, painting, music, architecture, oratory, can effect, ceases to satisfy and please—When the eager chase after wealth flags, and beauty itself becomes a loathing—and when all worldly or carnal or æsthetic, or even scientific values, having done their office to the human character, and ministered their part to its development—then, if not before, comes forward this overarching thought and brings its eligibilities, germinations. Most neglected in life of all humanity's attributes, easily covered with crust, deluded and abused, rejected, yet the only certain source of what all are seeking, but few or none find—in it I for myself clearly see the first, the last, the deepest depths and highest heights of art, of literature, and of the purposes of life. I say whoever labors here, makes contributions here, or best of all sets an incarnated example here, of life or death, is dearest to humanity—remains after the rest are gone."[6]

The Quaker hush and quiet and the whisper of the infinite Presence are never altogether absent from Whitman's life, and they are unmistakable factors in much of his poetry.

There was, moreover, as I have said, a decided tendency to mystical experience in the psychological bent of his being. Like Socrates, he falls naturally into long continued silence, during which he seems to feel the pulsations of a deeper World throbbing through him—what he calls "the eternal beats, eternal systole and dyastole of life in things—wherefrom," he says, "I feel and

---

[6] Whitman's *Prose Works*, p. 476.

know that death is real beginning." "In such devout hours," he declares "(significant only because of the *me* in the center) creeds, conventions fall away and become of no account" before the simple idea of *identity*, that is, of mystical union.[7]

There are many references throughout his prose writings to what must have been personal experiences of this *identity*. "Only," he says in "Democratic Vistas," "only in perfect uncontamination and solitariness, only in meditation, devout ecstasy and soaring flight, does the soul solve its eternal problems. It is when the individual is alone that *identity* is felt—and the soul emerges. Alone in silent thought and awe and aspiration—and then the interior consciousness, like a hitherto unseen inscription, in magic ink, beams out its wondrous lines to sense. Bibles may convey, and priests expound, but it is exclusively for the noiseless operation of one's isolated Self to enter the pure ether of veneration, reach divine levels and commune with the unutterable."[8]

---

[7] These quoted words are taken from passages in *Cosmic Consciousness*, pp. 189–190.

[8] This passage is given in abbreviated form from *Prose Works* (1897), pp. 233–234.

There is an extraordinary description, full of sudden ejaculations, in "Specimen Days," of a great experience, which swept over him while he was watching the stars on a summer night in 1878. He calls the experience "Hours for the Soul." "I am convinced," he says, "there are hours of Nature, especially of the atmosphere, mornings and evenings, addressed to the Soul." Then follows his own experience: "There, in abstraction and stillness (I had gone off by myself to absorb the scene, to have the spell unbroken), the copiousness, the removedness, vitality, loose-clear-crowdedness, of that stellar concave spreading overhead, softly absorbed into me, rising so free, interminably high, stretching east, west, north, south—and I, though but a point in the center below, embodying all.

"As if for the first time, indeed, creation noiselessly sank into and through me its placid and untellable lesson, beyond—O, so infinitely beyond!—anything from art, books, sermons, or from science, old or new. The spirit's hour—religion's hour—the visible suggestion of God in space and time—now once definitely indicated, if never again.

The untold pointed at—the heavens all paved with it. The Milky Way, as if some superhuman symphony, some ode of universal vagueness, disdaining syllable and sound—a flashing glance of Deity, addressed to the soul. All silently—the indescribable night and stars—far off and silently."[9]

Here, as usual with Whitman, the *Soul* is the all-important fact. "I believe in you my soul," is a kind of refrain throughout the poet's life. He declares: "I will not make a poem, nor the least part of a poem, but has reference to the Soul." To *"loaf and invite my soul"* is his main theme in *Leaves of Grass,* and it is, for long stretches of his life, occupation enough for him. It might be well in our over-busy and over-material world if more Americans felt a call to get free from the storm and stress of life, the whirl and dance, to "invite the soul" and to learn with Whitman to "believe in the soul."

Still another passage from "Specimen Days," one of the most eloquent Whitman ever wrote, could have been written only by a person who had enjoyed, at least in high moments, something that corresponds to

[9] *Prose Works,* pp. 118–119.

"cosmic consciousness," or to the inflooding of the Oversoul: "There is, apart from mere intellect, in the make-up of every superior human identity (in its moral completeness, considered as *ensemble,* not for that moral alone, but for the whole being, including physique), a wondrous something that realizes without argument, frequently without what is called education (though I think it the goal and apex of all education deserving the name)—an intuition of the absolute balance, in time and space, of the whole of this multifarious, mad chaos of fraud, frivolity, hoggishness—this revel of fools, and incredible make-believe and general unsettledness, we call *the world;* a soul-sight of that divine clue and unseen thread which holds the whole congeries of things, all history and time, and all events, however trivial, however momentous, like a leashed dog in the hand of the hunter. Such soul-sight and root-center for the mind—mere optimism explains only the surface or fringe of it."[10]

Intimations of profound experiences are frequent in Whitman's poetry. They are

---
[10] *Prose Works,* p. 174.

an essential part of his life. They flash in as so many other things do, without dates or labels. They are elusive and hard to catch. But it is not too much to claim, I think, that it was precisely these transcending experiences that made him a poet. More than most of us he felt the reality of the Beyond, had *flashes* of insight that came unsought, and he *arrived* without knowing the steps and sequences which carried him on. A few lines, written in 1865, indicate how much he preferred mystical intuition to the slow precisions of discursive thought:

"When I heard the learned astronomer;
  When the proofs, the figures, were ranged in columns before me;
  When I was shown the charts and the diagrams, to add, divide, and measure them;
  When I, sitting, heard the astronomer, where he lectured with much applause in the lectureroom,
  How soon, unaccountable, I became tired and sick;
  Till rising and gliding out, I wandered off by myself,
  In the mystical moist night-air, and from time to time,
Looked up in perfect silence at the stars."

But by far the most revealing single passage which Whitman ever wrote, either in poetry or prose, is a personal account of the invasion of the Larger Life into his inmost being, leaving him transformed, in some sense reborn, by the experience. Nobody else in the world would have described a mystical experience in this strange fashion, but the outstanding fact is clear through the elusive words that a spiritual reality greater than his own self enswathed him and embraced him and penetrated to the very heart of him and brought to him a new epoch of existence. Let me quote here the strange account, in which he is addressing the invading *Soul:*

"I mind how once we lay, such a transparent summer morning;
How you settled your head athwart my hips, and gently turned over upon me,
And parted the shirt from my bosom bone, and plunged your tongue to my bare-stript heart,
And reached till you felt my beard, and reached till you held my feet.
Swiftly arose and spread around me the peace and knowledge that pass all the argument of earth;

And I know that the hand of God is the promise of my own,
And I know that the Spirit of God is the brother of my own;
And that all the men ever born are also my brothers, and the women my sisters and lovers;
And that a kelson of the creation is love."[11]

This experience occurred apparently in the summer before he wrote *Leaves of Grass,* and after it he "wandered amazed at his own lightness and glee." He reached an elation that nothing could disturb and attained an optimism that rose triumphant over evil and over death.

"All goes onward and outward, nothing collapses;
And to die is different from what anyone supposed, and luckier."

. . . .

"I know I am deathless,
I know this orbit of mine cannot be swept by a carpenter's compass."

The whole universe seemed to him crammed with beauty and with miracle and everything makes its particular revelation of the Divine.

---
[11] *Leaves of Grass.*

"I believe a leaf of grass is no less than the journey-work of the stars,
And the pismire is equally perfect, and a grain of sand, and the egg of the wren,
And the tree-toad is a chef-d'œuvre for the highest,
And the running blackberry would adorn the parlors of heaven,
And the narrowest hinge in my hand puts to scorn all machinery,
And the cow crunching with depress'd head surpasses any statue,
And a mouse is miracle enough to stagger sextillions of infidels."

He felt that his soul reached below "the soundings of plummets." He entered so profoundly into the life of things—the heart of the cosmos—that he seemed to bear and to share the sorrows and the crucifixions of the ages. In fact, he entered so profoundly and so sympathetically into the life and the struggles of humanity that he was as a result peculiarly fitted to do the immense work of love for the suffering and dying soldiers in the hospitals during the Civil War. He was always a lover of little children and they felt almost instantly his gentleness, his kindness, and his comrade-spirit. Only a tender soul, rich in genuine love, could have written the words:

"The little one sleeps in its cradle;
 I lift the gauze, and look a long time, and silently brush away flies with my hand."

In some real sense he became *identified* with the suffering heart of man and travailed in spirit with those who wept in sorrow and who sweat with toil:

"Agonies are one of my changes of garments,
 I do not ask the wounded person how he feels. I myself become the wounded person,
 My hurts turn livid upon me as I lean on a cane and observe."

"Not a mutineer walks handcuffed to jail but I am handcuffed to him and walk by his side."

"Not a cholera patient lies at the last gasp, but I also lie at the last gasp;
 My face is ash-colored—my sinews gnarl—away from me people retreat."

The *identity* experience of which Whitman has so much to say is always a *double-identity*. He feels himself united always with the Above as well as with the below. He reaches down in tenderness and love to human sufferers just because he feels himself to be in some real sense an organ of a larger Love than his own. It is in this upper *identity* that what is properly called his "mysticism" mainly consists. He says quite plainly that he has seen "A sudden gleam divine, precipitating, bursting all these bubbles, fashions, wealth."

And again:

> "As in a swoon, one instant,
> Another sun, ineffable full-dazzles me,"

and heaven and God seem as real to him as the East River and the well-known Brooklyn ferry-boat.

He feels himself in vivid moments to be "Walking the old hills of Judæa, with the beautiful gentle God by my side." The visible and the invisible meet and kiss one another: "The palpable is in its place, and the impalpable in its place," and one of them is felt to be just as essential to the universe as the other is—"the unseen is proved by the seen."

"I say," he declares, "the whole earth, and all the stars in the sky, are for Religion's sake."

"I say no man has ever been half devout enough;
None has ever yet adored or worshiped half enough;
None has begun to think how divine he himself is, and how certain the future is."

In a beautiful figure of parental love, drawing upon experiences with his father, the poet of *Leaves of Grass*, still conscious of the invasion of the divine and of encompassing spiritual presence, says:

"Not he, with a daily kiss, onward from childhood kissing me
Has winded and twisted around me that which holds me to him
Any more than I am held to heaven, to the spiritual world."

There can be little doubt, I suppose, that in the rapture and ecstasy of this early experience, Whitman was swept on into a pantheistic conception of the universe and of life. In the light of this absorption of the particular into the All, the old landmarks between good and evil become for the moment blurred for him. Everything is good and nothing is evil. He considers, he says, "a curl of smoke or a hair on the back of my hand, just as curious as any revelation." It is, however, in spite of the infallible air with which he says it, a dangerous and an unsound point of view. Some revelations are much greater than others. Poets and mystics and a few philosophers have slid into this way of thinking—particularly in their youth and in the days of yeast and ferment. It will not do, however, for a philosophy of life. It cost Whitman heavily and it delayed for years the recognition which he deserved. He was, I believe, essentially clean and pure of soul. He was as tender toward every other woman in the world as he was toward his mother, but most of his readers did not know that. They thought he was coarse and impure, and many still think so.

One can hardly read *Leaves of Grass*, from which most of the above quotations are taken, with one's eyes open without seeing that the writer of it has had what the mystics call "a flash." The world has become for him, as Whitman describes it, "a melange of the seen and unseen." He has not yet at thirty-five attained the calm poise and power that were to be his later in life. He is at this stage in the throes of creating birth, he feels "the procreant urge of the world," working tumultuously in him, but one thing is pretty clear and certain, even at this stage, and that is, that the poet is conscious of some stupendous Life and Power—a Great Companion and Comrade of his soul—working like a leaven of life through him. The note of joy which he beat out into music in 1870 triumphantly expresses what he had long felt:

"Joy! shipmate—joy!
 (Pleased to my Soul at death I cry);
 Our life is closed—our life begins;
 The long, long anchorage we leave,
 The ship is clear at last—she leaps!
 She swiftly courses from the shore;
 Joy! shipmate—joy!"

The poems of this radiant period are significantly "dedicated to the Invisible World," and in one of them come these words:

"Lover Divine and Perfect Comrade!
 Waiting, content, invisible yet, but certain,
 Be thou my God."

This is the period in which he wrote "Passage to India," a poem of great power, which is full of mystical reverie and prophetic flashes. He once said of himself: "There is more of me, the essential, ultimate me, in that poem than in any of the [other] poems." "We can wait no longer!" he cries enthusiastically.

"We too take ship, O Soul!
  Joyous we too launch out on trackless seas!
  Fearless, for unknown shores, on waves of ecstasy
      to sail,
  Amid the wafting winds (thou pressing me to
      thee, I thee to me, O Soul),
  Caroling free—singing our song of God,
  Chanting our chant of pleasant exploration."

"Bear me, indeed, as through the regions infinite,
  Whose air I breathe, whose ripples hear—lave me
      all over;
  Bathe me, O God, in thee—mounting to thee,
  I and my soul to range in range of thee."

God is for him no far off mystery, no dim first cause. He is the spiritual reservoir of Life, the fountain of Truth and Beauty and Love, the pulse of all noble striving. He is the surrounding sea of Life into which the poet plunges like a joyous swimmer—*Bathe me, O God, in thee—lave me all over*. The whole poem throbs and thrills with the joy of living. The poet enters into the mystical inheritance of India, "doubles the Cape of Good Hope to some purpose," visits the "cradle of man," reads the Bibles of the early race, "the tremendous epics," feels the love and fire of "old occult Buddha," "cuts all his hawsers," shakes out every reef and, "with daring joy," "sails all the seas of God."

"Sail forth! Steer for the deep waters only!
  Reckless, O soul, exploring, I with thee and thou with me;
For we are bound where mariner has not yet dared to go,
And *we will risk the ship, ourselves and all.*"

It is not the mysticism of the great Christian saints. He knows little of the great mystics of history. He is always more concerned to *start* something than to repeat or copy the past. What one really finds in Whitman is the rapture, the thrill and wonder of a joyous, naïve soul, whose whole being floods with life and light, and who feels in great moments the tides of God's ocean of spiritual reality sweeping back into the channel of his own individual stream of life—and suddenly he is ready to venture ship and cargo and helmsman out on the high sea!

No one of Whitman's poems reveals the interior deeps of his life to quite the same extent as does the "Prayer of Columbus," first printed in 1871. It represents Columbus as "a battered wrecked old man," "stiff with many toils," and "nigh to death." The discoverer is on his last voyage, alone on the beach of one of the Antilles which he has discovered. The hulls of his ships are in the distance. His life, so full of promise once, now seems to be a failure and a defeat. Only God is left to the lonely soul, still majestic in his faith and his confidence. It is perfectly evident, however, that this is the experience and the prayer not of an explorer of the Antilles in the dawn of the sixteenth century, but of a religious and mystical soul, courageously facing the deepest issues of life, in the second half of the nineteenth century. It is the testimony of Whitman's own soul. Point for point the prayer tallies with the scenery and circumstance of the poet's inner and outer condition when the poem was written. Take these revealing words:

"Thou knowest the prayers and vigils of my youth;
Thou knowest my manhood's solemn and visionary meditations;
Thou knowest how, before I commenced, I devoted all to come to thee;
Thou knowest I have in age ratified all those vows, and strictly kept them;
Thou knowest I have not once lost nor faith nor ecstasy in thee."

These slow, weighty lines are deep with meaning. They remind one of Emerson's confession of faith in *Terminus*, where he also insists that he is obeying the *same Voice at eve* that he obeyed *at prime*. The poet insists not only that he has been faithful to his vision, but that the "ecstasy" which broke in upon his early manhood has remained as a controlling and guiding factor of his later life. There follow, in a like solemn strain, the noble words through which the poet declares the prophetic mission of his life and testifies that he has been the recipient of sealed orders from above. The passage is brief but striking:

"Oh, I am sure they really come from thee!
The urge, the ardor, the unconquerable will,

The potent, felt, interior command, stronger than
    words,
A message from heaven whispering to me even in
    sleep,
These sped me on."

But beyond all questions of mission, of plans, of emprises, of success or failure, is the passion in the prayer for God himself. Whether the young man was a mystic or not, the old gray poet certainly is:

"I cannot rest, O God—I cannot eat or drink or
    sleep,
  Till I put forth myself, my prayer once more to
    thee,
  *Breathe, bathe myself once more in thee—com-
    mune with thee,"*
"That thou, O God, my life hast lighted,
  With ray of light, steady, ineffable vouchsafed of
    thee,
  (Light rare, untellable—lighting the very light!
  Beyond all signs, descriptions, languages)
  For that, O God, be it my latest word—here on
    my knees,
  Old, poor and paralyzed—I thank thee."

Nobody can read those words without a silent thrill. The writer of them has made his contacts with a World that finger-tips do not touch. He has discovered, not new islands or a new continent, but, rather, a whole new universe of Life and Spirit. "Newer, better worlds, their mighty parturition."

"These things I see suddenly—
  As if some miracle, some hand divine, unseal'd my eyes."

After that there are no doubts, no halting, no fears. Death had never affrighted him; now it is only a happy episode in the life and the voyaging of a brave adventurer.

"Praised be the fathomless universe
  For life and joy, and for objects and knowledge curious,
  And for love, sweet love— But praise! praise! praise!
  For the sure-enwinding arms of cool-enfolding death."

That jubilant note is worthy to be put alongside of St. Francis' joyous welcome to "Sister Death."

I have been convinced, as I have studied the life and writings of this unique man and poet, that his triumphant attitude in the face of everything that confronted him—life and death, poverty and paralysis, things present and things to come—was due primarily to his first-hand conviction, his absolute certainty of an inner spiritual World of Life and Love which overbrims the world of atoms and molecules. He could say quite calmly in the power and demonstration of it:

"At the last, tenderly,
  From the walls of the powerful, fortressed house,
  From the clasp of the knitted locks, from the
      keep of the well-closed doors,
  Let me be wafted.
  Let me glide noiselessly forth;
  With the key of softness unlock the locks—with
      a whisper
  Set ope the doors, O Soul."

VII

MYSTICAL LIFE AND THOUGHT IN AMERICA

There is a widespread idea current in the world that "America" is a word synonymous with "practicality." It is assumed that we are dollar-chasers pure and simple, and are interested only in what we can get our hands on, to have and to hold. There are such Americans no doubt, and there are persons with like propensities in other countries and on other continents. But nobody knows America when he knows it only as a land of dollar-chasers and griffins who live in order to grasp. That is an unfair appraisal. It is a land of idealists as well as a land of huge bank accounts.

There is a strong spiritual strain in our composite blood. We rise naturally to the call of duty. We quickly feel the appeal to help to build a better world for unborn generations. We are like Jacob of old; we can see where lies our main chance for good returns, and yet on occasion we too can see angels, as he did, and feel them tugging at us, to pull our better self free.

Carlyle said once, inculcating his practical gospel of work, that "it is better to build a dog hutch than to dream of building a palace." Keep your feet on the ground and get something *done,* even if it is the puniest and most infinitesimal thing, rather than glow and thrill over sky domes and rainbow arches.

It all depends on what we are here for and what our central task really is. In any case a true and noble life must move on both these legs and not a single one of them alone. The practical attitude is an essential trait of life if one is to have coherence and guiding purpose and moral discipline in his character. The dreamer, the rainbow-chaser, who is only that, is a futile person. Someone asked President Lincoln once how long a man's legs ought to be, and the tall, awkward man humorously replied that they ought to be long enough to reach the ground! So they ought. And yet it is a poor type of person who never rises above the dull level of the earth and flings himself uncalculatingly at a seemingly impossible goal. Carlyle's dog-hutch practicality is, I am sure, unsound as a policy of life. I would not advocate as a substitute for it a life of futile dreaming of a palace never actually built. But I believe it is distinctly better to begin to build a temple which rises in dream and vision beyond our power to finish in any temporal period than it is to be content with a pine wood, easily finished dog hutch. The first thing to consider and to insist upon is some kind of a structure that has a holy place in it, and just the absence of that shekinah is the fatal defect of the easy practicality of a dog hutch philosophy and mad dollar chasing. We cannot build a great America on the practical utilitarian plane alone. That sort of structure will some day collapse with even greater ruin than the moral debacle of Europe during the terrible years from 1914 to 1918.

It will be well for us, if we look seriously to see whether the holy place is an inherent part of our building plans. If it is not, our vast educational program and our extraordinary scientific discoveries and our economic progress will only make the collapse the more terrible when "the Doom from its worn sandals shakes the dust against our land." This deeper side of our American life has never at any epoch of our history been altogether wanting. The ships that brought the early colonists were steered to these shores by a high and living faith and by the vision of unseen realities.

From its early colonial period in the seventeenth century there has always been an important mystical strand in the life and thought of America. Members of the small mystical sects of the English Commonwealth (1640-1660) came to various sections of the American colonies in the hope of finding larger freedom of thought and they transmitted their ideals and aspirations to their successors.

The Quakers began to *invade* America from 1656 onward and they gave expression in their silent meetings to a mystical form of worship and in their practical experiments to a philosophy of life which had drawn heavily upon the great mystics of the historic church. Whittier has given us in his "Pennsylvania Pilgrim" a beautiful word picture of Quaker worship at its best as a form of living communion with God:

"Lowly before the Unseen Presence knelt
Each waiting heart, till haply some one felt
On his moved lips the seal of silence melt.

"Or, without spoken word, low breathings stole
Of a diviner life from soul to soul
Baptizing in one tender thought the whole."

A colony of Labadists (followers of Jean de Labadie) settled in Maryland on the Bohemia River, near the head of Chesapeake Bay, in 1684, and these Flemish mystics contributed another element to the religion of America.

The Dutch and German sects that came to Pennsylvania in succession from 1684 to the middle of the eighteenth century brought a strong infusion of pietism and with it a great variety of types of mystical thought, at its best showing the influence of John Tauler and Jacob Boehme, and at its worst confused with a blend of mediæval theosophy and the Kabbalah.

Jonathan Edwards (1703-1758), who was probably the greatest theologian and one of the greatest philosophers America has produced, was perhaps the most notable American mystic of the eighteenth century. As in

Saint Augustine, so in Jonathan Edwards there were two men, the logical theologian and the intense mystic palpitating with awe and wonder over the direct experience of God. Edwards felt himself on a certain occasion in his youth to be swallowed up in God and brought into conjunction with his divine majesty and grace. The whole world seemed to him to be altered and to be filled with divine glory. His wife, Sarah Pierrepont, was too, from her early youth, a deeply gifted mystic.

Thomas C. Upham (1799-1872), professor of moral philosophy at Bowdoin College in Maine, made an extensive contribution to mystical thought in New England during the first half of the nineteenth century. He wrote a *Life of Madame Guyon* (1847), largely constructed out of her own autobiography and her other writings together with an added account of Fénelon. He wrote also a *Life of Catharine Adorna,* that is, Catharine of Genoa (1856). Three of his other books are essentially mystical, namely, *The Life of Faith* (1848), *The Interior Life* (1846) and *A Treatise on Divine Union* (1851). These books found their way into a great many homes and turned the thoughts of their readers in the direction of the mystical life.

The nineteenth century began with a dry rationalism in the ascendancy, in many quarters running out into arid deism. The reaction from this rationalism was quite naturally a counter wave of romanticism, as was the case in England and on the Continent of Europe. Coleridge's influence was a powerful factor in melting the rigid ice and in bringing a new vernal equinox. Still more important though less direct was the influence of Kant and the post-Kantian German philosophy, which came to America, at first, second-hand. An American translation of Cousin's *Introduction to the History of Philosophy* was an epoch-making book. It was a highly colored interpretation, but it worked like yeast on many susceptible minds. F. H. Hedge's *German prose Writers* was another source of inspiration. Schleiermacher and Goethe each had a few choice readers in New England, and they made their significant contribution. A little later came the powerful influence of Thomas Carlyle.

It was Ralph Waldo Emerson (1803-1882) who seized these various lines of influence and formed out of them all a new blend of thought which was predominantly mystical. Emerson is, I think, America's foremost mystic in range of influence. Besides the romantic and post-Kantian influences Emerson was profoundly influenced by Plato, and even more by Plotinus, both of whom he studied in Thomas Taylor's English translations. Jacob Boehme, or "Behmen," as he called him, and George Fox were also very much in evidence as sources in Emerson's mysticism. Emerson's lectures given in most American cities and his winged essays and poems carried his interpretation of life and thought into multitudes of homes, and it became a mighty leaven in the general life of America. Emerson's essay on "The Oversoul" is the most fresh, natural, and spontaneous piece of mystical writing we have yet produced. "The soul's communication of truth," he wrote, "is the highest event in nature . . . and this communication is an influx of the Divine Mind into our mind. It is an ebb of the individual rivulet before the flowing surges of the sea.

. . . Every moment when the individual feels invaded by it is memorable." "There is no bar," again he says, "or wall in the soul, where man, the effect, ceases and God, the cause, begins. The walls are taken away. We lie open on one side to the deeps of spiritual nature, to the attributes of God." This same Life that bursts into man with an invading revealing force also pours itself through nature, which thus becomes the garment that half reveals and half conceals the Spirit that weaves the world. This is the mystical message of that haunting poem of Emerson, "The Sphinx":

> "Uprose the merry Sphinx,
>   And crouched no more in stone;
> She melted into purple cloud,
>   She silvered in the moon;
> She spired into a yellow flame;
>   She flowered in blossoms red;
> She flowed into a foaming wave;
>   She stood Monadnoc's head.
> Through a thousand voices
>   Spoke the universal dame:
>   'Who telleth one of my meanings
> Is master of all I am.' "

It is often asked whether Plotinus and

Eckhart were pantheists. They were not quite complete pantheists, but they were always close to it, and so, too, was Emerson. The line of division is hard to draw, but all these mystics believed that God was transcendent as well as immanent, and they all believed in the reality of personal differentiation.

Walt Whitman (1819-1892), next to Emerson, has been the most impressive literary interpreter of mysticism in America, and his autobiographical passages plainly reveal the fact that he was himself in his own personal experiences a mystic of remarkable depth. There are many passages in Whitman's prose which either report direct mystical experiences or interpret the nature and value of mysticism. But by far the most important contributions that he has made in this field are to be found in his poems.

Whitman's friend, Dr. R. M. Bucke (1837-1901), of Canada, wrote a book that has had a distinct influence on mysticism in American thought. It was entitled *Cosmic Consciousness* and was published in 1900. Another Canadian, George John Blewett, published in 1907 an illuminating volume on

The Study of Nature and the Vision of God, which contains much that is in the mystical line, or at least of value to mystics.

There is a mystical note in many of the poems of John Greenleaf Whittier, who was a Quaker in faith and practice, and who always put a strong emphasis on the inward life and on direct experience of God. James Russell Lowell in his letters reports more than one occasion when his life seemed to be invaded with a Divine Presence and there are strong traces of mysticism in his poetry, especially in "The Cathedral."

Next in importance, however, after Emerson and Whitman comes William James (1842-1910). He claimed not to have been a mystic himself—"my own constitution shuts me out from the enjoyment of mystical experiences"—but his *Letters* would indicate that there was a strong mystical tendency in him. In any case he was a sympathetic and penetrating interpreter of mysticism and of mystics. His *Varieties of Religious Experience* (1902), in spite of some striking defects, has stimulated hosts of readers and has given the world a very interesting interpretation of mysticism in terms of the subliminal life of man. William James brought into prominent notice, through an article in the *Hibbert Journal* for July, 1910, a very interesting American mystic named Benjamin Paul Blood, whom James called "a pluralistic mystic" (see *Memories and Studies*). Josiah Royce in his Gifford Lectures, *The World and the Individual* (1900-1901), has devoted two profoundly important chapters to "The Mystical Interpretation" and to "The Outcome of Mysticism." They are full of insight and wisdom. Royce has also an illuminating chapter on "Meister Eckhart" in his volume, *Studies of Good and Evil* (1898).

My own *Studies in Mystical Religion* was first issued in 1909, preceded by a number of briefer interpretations. *Spiritual Reformers in the Sixteenth and Seventeenth Century*, which has been translated into German, followed in 1914. It contains a study of a group of neglected mystics with a critical introductory chapter on the nature of mysticism. *New Studies in Mystical Religion* was published in 1927.

In 1912 Professor William Ernest Hocking, of Harvard, then of Yale, published his immensely important book, *The Meaning of God in Human Experience*. It is among the major contributions that have been made to mystical study in America. Charles A. Bennett, of Yale University, a former student of Professor Hocking's, has carried forward the philosophical study of mysticism in a very important book entitled *A Philosophical Study of Mysticism* (1923). Professor James B. Pratt, of Williams College, is another notable American contributor to the interpretation of mysticism. His most important work in this field will be found in the last four chapters of his book, *Religious Consciousness* (1920). Professor James Leuba, of Bryn Mawr College, is one of the best known of all American writers on mysticism. He has contributed many critical articles on the subject and he has made a searching psychological study of mysticism in his *Psychology of Religious Mysticism* (1925). Professor Leuba's position is critical and destructive of the objective religious value of mysticism. Professor William P. Montague, of Columbia, has an excellent chapter on "The Method of Mysticism" in his book, *The Ways of Knowing* (1925). Professor W. H. Seldon, of Yale, has a valuable section on "Intuitionism and Mysticism" in his book, *Strife of Systems*, which was published in 1918. In 1915 John Wright Buckham published a small book entitled *Mysticism and Modern Life,* which has been widely read and has had a marked influence on mystical thought. Another interpretative book of real value is by Charles Morris Addison on *The Theory and Practice of Mysticism* (1918). In 1914 Dr. Margaret L. Bailey published an important Doctor's Thesis on *Milton and Jacob Boehme.* Margaret Prescott Montague has published a charming essay, describing her own experience in *Twenty Minutes of Reality* (1917). Mention should be made also of a little book by Katharine F. Pedrick with the title, *The Practical Mystic* (1915). In 1921 E. Hershey Sneath, of Yale University, edited a volume of Essays on the mystical element in various historical leaders of religious thought. The chapters are written by well-known American authors. The collection of Essays bears the title *At One With the Infinite.* I have just been reading a charming and penetrating little book by a Mexican mystic, born on the Western Pacific coast. It is by Amando Nervo and it bears the beautiful title, *Plenitude*. It is happily translated by William F. Rice. It is full of the joy of life and is a book of serenity and optimism.

In the field of what the Germans call "Mysticismus," or Pseudo-mysticism, the output in America has been very large and the list of books and articles would be a long one, but I have professed to cover in this brief review only the purer types of mysticism, and that with no claim to completeness. This outline of the contributions to the mystical life seems small when compared with the contribution that has been made in Germany or France or Italy, or even England, where there has always been a dearth of prophetic leaders and where the prevailing note of philosophy has been that of a practical common-sense view. England has given us in this century four outstanding interpreters of mystical religion who have profoundly influenced and are influencing our American life and thought. They are Baron Friedrich von Hügel, Evelyn Underhill, Dean W. R.

Inge and Dom Cuthbert Butler, in his *Western Mysticism*. This outline hardly touches below the surface. The current of mystical life and thought is by no means truly revealed in any review of the books that deal with the subject. There are hundreds of mute and unnamed mystics for every one who writes a book. In fact, the most important interpreters of mysticism in all periods are those persons who quietly practice the presence of God in their daily lives without even being conscious that they are rare and unusual persons and often without knowing the meaning of the word "mystic."

Lord Rosebery, in his fine estimate of Oliver Cromwell, called him "a practical mystic," which he defined as "a man who has inspiration and adds to it the energy of a mighty man of action"—"a man who has a Sinai of his own." Abraham Lincoln is a notable instance of an American practical mystic of this type who had both a Sinai and a Golgotha of his own. We now know that he passed through an arid period of deism in his earlier life and one can trace the slow growth of a deeper religious life forming at the roots of his being as he came into the constructive period of his political career. But even when this deepened life had become formed as an indubitable fact, Lincoln said very little that revealed in words the nature of his deep-rooted faith. The type of Lincoln's religion has been the subject of many debates. His solemn references to God became an impressive feature of his speeches and letters as the stern task of his life grew clear and as the shadows thickened across his path. The greatest speech of his life—the one at Gettysburg in 1863—contains a phrase that was not in the original draft of the address. "We here highly resolve that these dead shall not have died in vain and that this nation, *under God,* shall have a new birth of freedom." The phrase, "under God," either broke in spontaneously as Lincoln was speaking, or was jotted in on his early draft as he sat on the platform. In any case it represents that silent inward push of Divine power which he had come to feel working in his life. The remarkable quality of the religious note in the "Second Inaugural" is clear to every reader. But there is a depth to it which goes down far under the written words, and that underlying experience of divine presence was, I believe, Lincoln's greatest asset on the hard road which his feet had to walk. He was in the best sense a practical mystic. In his great funeral oration over the martyred President, Henry Ward Beecher said, "His life now is grafted upon the Infinite and will be fruitful as no earthly life can be." It was just that quality of being grafted upon the Eternal and the Infinite during those last wonderful years of his life in Washington that made Abraham Lincoln the central power station of the whole country in its time of struggle and suffering.

Many persons have been surprised, though not all of us, to discover in a recent life of President Charles W. Eliot of Harvard that he too was a practical mystic. Dr. Francis G. Peabody wrote to him on his twenty-fifth anniversary as President of the University saying to him, "You are the man who, more than any other, shows me perpetually how to rely on the Eternal for personal strength." President Eliot replied: "I feel glad that what has been, I believe, a fact in my inner life these thirty years past has been visible to a close observer of my official career." His biographer rightly declares that religion was his "major interest" and that "he had a first-hand experience of the living God." But this "abiding consciousness of being linked with God" did not appear in his written or spoken words; it came out in action as the driving power of the great educator's life and service.

Samuel F. B. Morse is another example of one of the foremost Americans who was throughout the years of his creative work a practical mystic, translating into action and invention a faith in God which was as deep as his life. The first half of his life was devoted to art, and he had put himself by 1835 very close to the top of American painters. By what now seems like a sheer caprice of ill fortune he lost the expected government commission to paint one of the historical panels in the rotunda of the new Capitol at Washington. He was deeply grieved by this blow, and by the failure of America to appreciate his artistic powers, but he quietly turned, without any loss of faith in himself or in God, to his other dominant interest, which was the perfection of a system of intercommunication by telegraph. His work in the new field was extraordinarily successful and he took his place in the little group of the world's supreme inventors. In all the labors that revealed his genius he was deeply concerned to be the organ and instrument of the spiritual energies of the universe as his telegraph key was the instrument for electrical energies. He was in life and spirit simple, childlike, humble, and unworldly. He told one of his friends once that "he felt as though he was doing a great work for God's glory as well as for man's welfare, and that this had been his long cherished thought." "His whole soul and heart," this friend writes, "appeared to be filled with a glow of love and goodwill, and his sensitive and impassioned nature seemed almost to transform him in my eyes into a prophet." We have in Samuel Morse, I think, a pretty plain case of a man who won his immortal place in the Hall of Fame by his inventive genius, but who, just as plainly, deserves by his sensitive spiritual life to be enrolled among the great practical mystics of America.

I think Alice Freeman Palmer stands in

my mind as nearest the ideal American woman of any in our national life. Other women were more famous leaders of causes. There have been others who were greater creative scholars and perhaps two more distinguished organizers and administrators. But I know of no one who has attained quite the completeness, perfection, charm, and beauty of personal character that were revealed in Alice Freeman Palmer. Here once more, as in the case of the three great Americans whom I have mentioned, her religion was essentially a practical mysticism. She had a way all through her life of making her decisions and choosing her course and giving herself in noble service "face to face with God," that is, as though she were in his visible presence and as acting positively for the love of God. It was his presence here in the world that made it for her a beautiful and glorious world to live in. She went about her life, her duties and her tasks with a sense of joyous at-homeness in her Father's world. God was for her a living reality that gave every feature of life its worth and its meaning, and so she lived a rich and wonderful life, shot through at every point by his life and love and made radiant and thrilling even when she was doing ordinary, commonplace things.

These four foremost Americans are typical of a very large number of persons, small and great, who have builded the moral and spiritual foundations of our national life and our social fabric. These builders have, of course, not all been mystics of any type. But wherever I go in America and stay long enough to know the people of any community in city or in rural sections, I always find some of these practical mystics. They have some hidden quality of life that raises the whole spiritual level of the community to which they belong. They walk among their neighbors in the quiet round of work and "wist not that their faces shine," but in actual fact they are the restorers of what has been called "the lost radiance of Christianity." They are as truly a demonstration of spiritual energies as a trolley car or a power house is a demonstration of electrical energies. They "broadcast" night and day by a radio method as old as the gospel Life-forces which bring new meaning to personal goodness and which create a more wholesome social atmosphere for the entire community to breathe.

There have, furthermore, been certain epochs of spiritual awakening in our American life when religion has been raised from a low-power to a high-power level in a great many persons' lives. Religion has passed over from a dull, static performance, gone through with mechanically, to a living, throbbing, revitalized power to live by. It has become first-hand instead of being merely second-hand. The reality of God and the saving power of Christ are *felt* as an experience and no longer merely talked about.

There are many ways of drawing upon the invisible resources of the universe and of releasing energy to live by. Religion is one of these ways. When a person succeeds, by conscious or subconscious processes, in unifying the usually divided will, in concentrating all the inner forces upon one absorbing end, in focusing the soul's aspiration and loyalty upon one central object which meets its needs and seems adequate for its nature, this surrender of self to a higher and holier Will produces the state and condition that are essential for the flooding in of spiritual energy and for an increment and re-enforcement of one's normal powers. Everybody knows through some memorable experience what it means to lose suddenly all fear and fear-thoughts that have obsessed him and to rise up with heightened courage to face the tasks that are waiting to be done. Most persons, sometime in their lives, have seen the shadows flee away, shot through by a conquering light, and have found themselves possessed with insight and forward looking, victorious spirit. The literature of conversion is full of records of men and women, beaten and defeated, down and out, suddenly lifted to new levels of experience, put within reach of transforming forces, flooded with transfiguring light, and becoming in the strength of this faith or experience "twice-born" persons.

This arrival of new forces of energy is, I believe, a distinguishing mark of first-hand religion, religion in its real intention. In other words, there are in brief two main types of religion, however disguised under names and forms. There is (1) religion in its intensified, dynamic quality, and (2) there is a religion which consists of a deposit or survival of conceptions or of practice, carried along because they have become sacred habits, traditions and customs, or because they are believed to have a utilitarian value. The difference is not in creed; it is in *caloric*. In one case certain ideas which, for the preacher, have become cold, inert and dead, are shuffled back and forth as mere counters. In the other case the ideas which are used are absolutely alive and throbbing with quickened vitality and power. That strange experience called faith—an inner vision of reality, an assent of soul, an apprehension of things not seen—makes all the difference between formality on the one hand and *élan vital* on the other.

How the heightened caloric is brought into operation, why inert ideas suddenly become dynamic, will always remain in part at least a mystery. Mutations on any level are hard to explain. But the cardinal element here is almost certainly the contagion of kindled, fused personalities. A few persons of rare gift find a source of life and power, and they prove to be extraordinary transmitters of spiritual light and heat to others, and the age is vivified. The same ideas which in their souls glow with the heat of intensified life have just before, and may once again, seem as ineffective as the craters of extinct volcanoes.

We find ourselves to-day gravely in danger of losing the sway and potency of the spiritual side of life and of hardening down to the material and secular aspect of things. On the one hand science has stressed the importance of that which may be measured, described, and explained and has discounted imponderable realities, and the drive and hustle of business have kept the mind focused on tangible and bankable results, and so, once more, the intangible assets of the soul have been thrust out of focus and in many lives have become unreal. As so often before in crises of spiritual deadness and aridity, the mystic comes to-day to bear his testimony to the reality of these neglected assets of life, these deeper values by which men live.

I believe that we are on the verge of a new epoch in the spiritual life. There is an immense spiritual hunger everywhere in evidence. It has become perfectly clear that man cannot *live* by bread alone, nor can he *live* by exact scientific conclusions about the phenomena of the universe; and some of our greater scientific leaders are coming to be found, like Saul, among the prophets.

As science pushes its researches back into the secrets of matter and into the mysteries of life, it becomes ever more obvious that the mathematical formulæ and equations and quantum theories and ergs which sound so learned are only pointers and symbols of more ultimate realities which overbrim all these space-time methods of interpretation. It may quite possibly turn out to be true that the deepest nature of the universe is more like the deepest nature in ourselves than like anything else in heaven or earth. And the old mystical principle that *like knows like* may perhaps take on a new and deeper meaning. We cannot *know* the truth of any reality until we can find a method that enables us to get beyond symbolic knowledge of it and to enter the inner flow of reality and to know by coming into fused relations with the object of our quest. We have always trusted this inner way of knowing in reference to the character and personality of our friends. The pounds avoirdupois, the spatial dimensions, the facial curves, the finger prints, are signs and symbols, no doubt, and we might still further conceivably secure an exact diagrammatic display of the neural waves in the brain cortex, but none of those symbolic manifestations really *give* us the friend we love and trust. We have another way of knowing our friends. It does not give us demonstrative, communicable knowledge, and yet we would stake our souls on our penetrative insight of the real character of the person whom we love.

We arrive at our appreciation of beauty in much the same way. It is not the way of logic or proof or description. Something in us fuses in with something beyond us and we "know" by a direct inner approach. Professor A. S. Eddington, in his extraordinary book, *The Nature of the Physical World,* which marks a new stage in present day religious thought, maintains the view that "the world-stuff behind the pointer readings [that is, the symbols] is of a nature continuous with the mind" (p. 331). If it is so, as I believe it is, then we might well expect that it would be possible for us on occasion to enter into the inner flow of the Spirit and to feel ourselves a living part of the larger Whole. Just that experience the mystic claims to have, and he comes to the world with the testimony that the pointer readings and the symbolic accounts of the universe fall far short of the inner Heart of Reality as spirit in us meets and communes with the wider Spirit in whom we live and move and have our being.

CPSIA information can be obtained
at www.ICGtesting.com
Printed in the USA
LVHW061523260422
717282LV00013B/595

9 781494 054571